PEOPLE RESOURCING

CIPD REVISION GUIDE

Dr. Ted Johns has been a CIPD Chief Examiner for about 20 years and is currently Chief Examiner for both People Resourcing and Managing People. He is an experienced author with a number of publishers.

Charles Leatherbarrow is a Senior Lecturer in HRM at Staffordshire University. He teaches a wide range of undergraduate and postgraduate HRM modules, including the CIPD People Resourcing module. Prior to his academic career, Charles worked for Shell for over 18 years as a Human Resources Consultant and Manager.

The Chartered Institute of Personnel and Development is the leading publisher of books and reports for personnel and training professionals, students, and all those concerned with the effective management and development of people at work. For details of all our titles, please contact the publishing department:

tel: 020-8263 3387

fax: 020-8263 3850

e-mail: publish@cipd.co.uk

The catalogue of all CIPD titles can be viewed on the CIPD website:

www.cipd.co.uk/bookstore

PEOPLE RESOURCING

CIPD REVISION GUIDE

TED JOHNS AND CHARLES LEATHERBARROW

Chartered Institute of Personnel and Development

Published by the Chartered Institute of Personnel and Development,
CIPD House, Camp Road, London, SW19 4UX

First published 2003

Designed and typeset by Pumpkin House, Cambridge

Printed in Great Britain by The Cromwell Press, Trowbridge, Wiltshire

British Library Cataloguing in Publication Data
A catalogue of this manual is available from the British Library

ISBN 1 84398 025 8

Chartered Institute of Personnel and Development,
CIPD House, Camp Road, London, SW19 4UX

Tel: 020 8971 9000   Fax: 020 8263 3333

Email: cipd@cipd.co.uk   Website: www.cipd.co.uk

Incorporated by Royal Charter   Registered Charity No. 1079797

CONTENTS

• PUBLISHER'S NOTE

This book has been jointly written by Dr. Ted Johns, the Chief Examiner for People Resourcing, and Charles Leatherbarrow. Dr. Johns was responsible for contributing the Preface and Chapters one and two, Charles Leatherbarrow for the remainder of the book.

PREFACE

The thinking performer in a contributor culture

In selecting what to write for the Preface I have chosen to address the philosophy that underpins the design and structure of the People Resourcing elective. You may have already come across the by-now fashionable aphorism, 'select for attitude and train for skill', which is meant to convey the idea that if you are an organisation which needs your employees to behave and think in particular ways (eg be enthusiastic towards customers), it is a lot easier to achieve that outcome if you recruit people with appropriate attitudes in the first place. It's certainly much harder to try to inculcate people with positive customer-facing attitudes after they've already joined you – as many organisations have found when they've tried to change their culture whilst coping with a new, competitive environment. After all, if you have people with the right attitudes, you can always train them to produce the necessary skills and knowledge.

The same applies to budding HR professionals, namely, that the right attitude to begin with is more important than the straightforward possession of knowledge. So, when you embark on your CIPD studies, and begin to address the obligations of the Professional Development Scheme, it is vital that (a) you understand what attitudes will be expected of you as you demonstrate your competencies, and (b) you also understand what actions on your part – in the examinations, in the assignments, in your CPD activities, and in your everyday conduct – will enable you to exhibit those attitudes in a thoroughly convincing fashion.

Simply by choosing to read this commentary you have taken a significant step towards your final success not only in this subject, People Resourcing, but also in the CIPD's Professional Development Scheme as a whole. This is because my remarks will focus on the concept of the 'thinking performer' so far as its relevance to the whole of the CIPD's professional standards is concerned, and will show what it means to be a 'thinking performer' and how you can translate the philosophy and attitudes behind the 'thinking performer' concept into your examination performance, your assignments, and of course, most importantly of all, into your day-to-day approach to your professional activities at work.

It is a truism to claim that we live in turbulent, fast-moving times (though some organisations are more turbulent and fast-moving than others). Now, as I write, the times are dangerous as well.

The evidence is in front of our eyes: war, the threat and reality of 'regime change' both in countries and companies, warnings about terrorism, and McDonalds recording its first losses for over 30 years. Now, we are told, Ford and General Motors in the USA are developing bullet-proof cars for sale to the general public. These vehicles will look the same as ordinary models, but they can withstand shots from a .44 calibre Magnum, they will have an airtight seal with an internal supply of oxygen in case of a chemical assault, and have plates of ballistic steel and a reinforced fuel tank.

More than ever, in the UK economy, we need 'thinking performers'. Professor Michael Porter of Harvard Business School, reporting on the performance of the UK economy in early 2003, pointed out that it is vital for us to move from 'competing on relatively low costs of doing business', which by and large is what this country has done for many years, to 'competing on unique value and innovation'. Trying to be successful in any business arena purely on the basis of low costs is a strategy that is ultimately counter-productive, because there is always somebody who can cut costs faster than you (eg by moving production to Eastern Europe or customer service operations to India), and there is always a point beyond which cost-cutting cannot be undertaken without serious harm to product quality and service delivery. Performing on the basis of cost, moreover, does not require people to be 'thinking performers': quite the contrary, it requires individuals to conform to the dictates of a predetermined process, it presupposes strict routines, and it seeks where possible to eliminate human beings altogether. Once organisations and economies seek to compete down the route of 'unique value and innovation', in Porter's phrase, then things have to change as far as people management and people leadership are concerned. Searching out 'unique value and innovation' depends on ideas, and ideas only come from people who are motivated, optimistic, resourceful and enthusiastic, who are prepared to use their initiative in furtherance of the organisation's vision, goals and objectives, and who are encouraged to go beyond the constraints of their job descriptions in order to 'think outside the box'.

The 'thinking performer', however, can only flourish in what I call a 'contributor culture'. A contributor culture looks the same as an ordinary organisation, at least to the casual observer, but like the new bullet-proof cars from Ford and General Motors, it has some special features. The contributor culture has its own internal oxygen supply (committed, enthusiastic thinking performers), a reinforced fuel tank (committed, enthusiastic customers), and plates of ballistic steel (a 'big idea').

Armed with these defences, a contributor culture can withstand anything the competition can throw at it. Even better, it can withstand anything the *world* can throw at it. In a feature about 'Business in Bad Times' (5 April 2003), *The Economist* said that one of the things successful companies do when business is tough is 'to listen harder to their customers ... Customers are likely to be going through hard times too, and they may well show their appreciation of special consideration with more than a smile'. Being a contributor culture at moments like this represents an asset of almost measureless value.

So what is a contributor culture all about? More specifically, how does it relate to the CIPD's vision of the thinking performer?

Any organisation should expect its people to do what they are paid to do. This is the nub of the problem. Too many organisations (even in this age of so-called 'lean and mean' performance) don't expect all that much. For many, absence 'control' consists of paying people a bonus simply for turning up. Incompetence and mediocrity, once permitted, can become endemic; managers administer, control and constrain, but cannot lead; jobs are specified in terms of tasks to be performed, not accountabilities to be achieved.

In the best-performing organisations, by contrast, people are valued principally for their outputs – for their contribution. What these contributor culture organisations have are people who:

- will go the extra mile, demonstrating 'organisational citizenship' and 'discretionary' behaviour through their flexibility, their willingness to go beyond their job description, and indeed their view that the job description represents a baseline for personal development rather than a ceiling for individual effort

- will 'add value', making a difference through active participation in continuous-improvement programmes, through their awareness of the 'big picture', and their readiness to ask awkward questions like 'Why do we …?' and 'Why don't we …?'

These are the kinds of people that the CIPD celebrates in its portrayal of the thinking performer as the central plank in the Professional Development Scheme platform.

People in organisations are expected to be both efficient and effective. Being *efficient* is about *doing things right* – obeying the rules, enforcing procedures, complying with the law, implementing standardised processes, and mouthing the words in the corporate script. Being *effective*, by contrast, is about *doing the right things* – delivering results that make a difference, adding value through incremental improvement, or even initiating a wholly transformational change.

Many companies measure the efficiency of their staff in the mistaken belief that in doing so they're also measuring effectiveness. Even now there are large numbers of customer-contact people in call centres who are incentivised by the need to achieve, say, a throughput of 40 phone calls per hour, and who are penalised if their performance falls below this magic figure. Yet call duration is (for the most part) not what matters to the customer. And is it not the case that the customer's needs, and the customer's experience, should drive what gets measured and therefore what gets done? What seems to happen in reality is that faced with the awkward dilemma of trying to measure the customer experience, managers will concentrate instead on measuring something that is easily measurable (call duration) in the – largely forlorn – hope that one metric (call duration) is correlated with another (customer satisfaction).

Thinking performers are people who do things right *and* do the right things. Further, they understand that if there is a conflict between the two, then doing the right thing (eg sending the customer away satisfied) may justifiably take precedence over doing things right (eg sticking to the strict letter of the law with regard to acceptance of returned goods). Above all, thinking performers are contributors:

- They perform in the sense that they deliver the day-to-day operational results expected from them.

- They 'add value' by reflecting about what is done and how it is done. For a thinking performer, it is not enough to be told that something 'has always been done that way'.

- Thinking performers are curious about and alert to the outside world, aware of ideas being developed and tried out in other organisations. For a thinking performer, what matters is whether it works, not whether it appears in a textbook.

- Thinking performers seek to support the 'big idea' and the 'big picture' for their organisation. Their perspective is generous, not mean, and their horizons are wide, not narrow.

- Thinking performers accept continuous learning as a regular, unsurprising expectation associated with their jobs and with their professional obligations within the CIPD.

For you to succeed in your studies and in the assessment systems associated with the CIPD's Professional Development Scheme, then assimilation of a thinking performer mentality is crucial. It may not be easy for you, especially if you are employed in an organisation that does not itself display a culture favourable to thinking performer attitudes, but you have to remember that the aim of the Professional Development Scheme is not primarily to train you to perform your current role for your existing employer more efficiently, but rather to prepare you for a multi-faceted future within the personnel/HR profession.

Dr Ted Johns

Chief Examiner, People Resourcing

May 2003

LIST OF FIGURES

• GENERAL EXAMINATION GUIDANCE

■ Introduction

To begin with, you should understand clearly the underpinning philosophical attitudes and values that the Chief Examiner and his team bring to the process of assessing your examination script. These have been discussed and outlined in my Preface to this Revision Guide, but they deserve to be re-emphasised here if only because they show that the criteria are not based on some whimsical preferences owned by the examiners, but are linked to the CIPD's strategic vision for itself (and for its members).

Examiners are expected to apply the '2+10+5' framework (see below) to the evaluation of each script as a whole and to the evaluation of each answer. Assessing a script holistically against the '2+10+5' yardsticks becomes crucial in the case of individuals at the borderline between Pass and Marginal Fail, and at the borderline between Fail and Marginal Fail. The critical question asked when considering these borderline issues is: 'Are we prepared to see this individual going out into the world armed with the professional imprimatur of the CIPD? Are they likely to perform in a manner which upholds both the vision of the CIPD and the strategic thinking performer aspirations of the Professional Development Scheme (PDS)?' If there is doubt about the response to this question, then a putative Pass may be downgraded to Marginal Fail, and so on.

To cite a precise example, the May 2003 examination paper in People Resourcing included a question asking students to summarise and explain the new employment rights that came into effect in April 2003, and another question that invited discussion about what the adjective 'good' might mean when applied to an organisation's employee. The vast majority of candidates, if selecting the employment rights question, were able to explore the topic at length and in depth, earning significant marks for themselves in the process. However, it was the other question – seeking views on what we might be visualising when we talk of someone as a 'good' employee – that really sought an expression of the thinking performer perspective, attitudes and values. For any candidate displaying marginal performance – a final mark hovering on the 48 or 49 level – what would make the difference, in determining an overall pass, would be a high-quality, thinking performer response to the 'good' employee question rather than a high-quality, comprehensive treatment for the question about new employment rights. The employment rights question requires a demonstration of up-to-date knowledge, and although that is important (indeed, it is why a question was asked about it in the examination), it is less important than possession of appropriate attitudes that are consistent with the '2+10+5' model.

- The 2 refers to the CIPD vision of the HR professional as a 'business partner' and a thinking performer. It is not necessary to rehearse here the arguments for a 'business partner' perspective, except to say that this has to be the way forward if the personnel/HR function is to be taken seriously, to exert significant influence in the organisation, to attract resources (physical, financial and human), and to offer exciting career opportunities to those entering it.

- The 10 are the ten competencies listed in the PDS literature: personal drive and effectiveness; people management and leadership; business understanding; professional and ethical behaviour; added-value result achievement; continuing learning; analytical and intuitive/creative thinking; 'customer' focus; strategic thinking; and communication, persuasion and interpersonal skills.

- The 5 are the five 'BACKUP' competencies linked specifically to the PDS assessment system: business focus; application capability; knowledge of the subject; understanding; and persuasion/presentation skills.

In case there should be any misunderstanding, moreover, the entire '2+10+5' framework is relevant to all those entering the PDS process, no matter how junior their position in any given organisation. Thus entry into professional membership of the CIPD presupposes the capacity for strategic thinking, a 'business partner' perspective, and a breadth of critical understanding (to take some parts of the framework as examples): students must be able to demonstrate the connections between even a junior role and the organisation's strategic goals; they should be able to show how their activities 'add value'; and that their operational thinking extends further than the existing, conventional practices used within their own sector or enterprise.

To illustrate answers that do not exemplify the '2+10+5' requirements, let us take one response to the May 2003 question about the meaning of 'good' when used in the context of people performance: 'They deliver what they are asked of in a timely manner. They are present at their desks for long hours. They do not bring lots of problems, so therefore they are easy maintenance. They are a likeable person.' There is no sense here of one who has absorbed a thinking performer perspective, or the notion of discretionary (organisational citizenship) behaviour, or the fashionable popularity of teamwork and group commitment. Indeed, the expectation that a 'good' employee will be present at his/her desk 'for long hours' is a manifestation of 'presenteeism' in action that is wholly antithetical to the pursuit of genuine employee excellence.

Another example may be cited from the November 2002 Employee Resourcing examination, which included a question about the 'select for attitude, train for skill' principle, inviting students to comment on its meaning and its potential application in their own environment. The opening paragraph from one answer reads as follows: 'My organisation is a local authority and have [sic] a very structured selection process based on qualifications, skills, experience and knowledge. This ensure [sic] that we meet our equal opportunity obligations and there is no discrimination against potential employees. "Recruit for attitude, train for skill" would certainly be contrary to our practices as "recruit for attitude" is quite subjective and can be open to discriminatory practices.'

This material is unacceptable for a number of reasons. First, it demonstrates no awareness of the approaches used in other organisations – in some other local authorities, let alone large, reputable and even world-class employers in the private sector (such as Asda, Tesco, Lands End Clothing, Nokia, First Direct, Microsoft, Pret-a-Manger, and Egg), where attitude is the key capability sought and where few successful accusations of discrimination have ever been advanced. Second, it assumes that the systems used in the local authority that employs this student could not possibly be changed or improved. Third, it is taken as axiomatic that the purpose of employee resourcing is to ensure that equal opportunity obligations are fulfilled and discrimination is avoided. But this is not so: the purpose of employee/people resourcing is to produce people who can willingly contribute to the furtherance of the organisation's goals and higher-order vision; legal/ethical compliance will not by itself enable this purpose to be achieved. Fourth, it is no argument against 'recruit for attitude, train for skill' to claim that it would be 'contrary' to the practices currently used in any given organisation. Students for the CIPD qualification are meant to be capable of assimilating and assessing new ideas for their potential value, irrespective of the degree to which these ideas are exhibited within existing procedures. This is what the thinking performer paradigm is crucially about.

I readily concede that there are many organisations that could not be characterised as a contributor culture and where the notion of all employees as thinking performers would not be regarded as either credible or attractive. When an examination question on the subject was presented to Employee Resourcing students in 2001 (before the thinking performer vision had become central to the CIPD's qualification system), some of the answers were universally depressing and negative:

- 'This vision [of the thinking performer] would not be achievable in my organisation: the senior management are authoritarian and like it that way.'

- 'What the senior managers say [in my organisation] is not challenged. There is little or no employee participation or involvement. People are expected to do as they are told. Anyone who has their thoughts on how to do anything keeps these thoughts to themselves.'

- '[Getting our people to act as thinking performers] would cost a vast amount of money and waste valuable time.'

- 'In a production environment, [thinking performers] would be counter-productive because of the insistence on strict routines, tight procedural controls and close supervision.'

Equally, pan-European research by the Gallup Organisation, reported in *People Management* ('What a waste' by Marcus Buckingham, 11 October 2001) has suggested that genuinely engaged employees (thinking performers) constitute only around 17 per cent of the workforce, with a further non-engaged group making up 63 per cent and the rest (20 per cent) being 'disengaged', alienated, cynical, negative, unco-operative and hostile.

I acknowledge that some CIPD students find themselves working in such enterprises, and must therefore have difficulties in adopting the thinking performer values. However, the continued existence of workplaces where people are expected merely to conform to prescribed routines, where they are never consulted, where they are treated in effect as 'commodities', only serves to reinforce the desirability of the thinking performer framework and its associated values.

■ What it takes to achieve success

To offer specific guidance when preparing for the People Resourcing examination I have chosen to highlight the five 'BACKUP' competencies and suggest some routes that will enable you to achieve (at a bare minimum) the necessary level of adequacy in your performance across all five: business focus, application capability, knowledge of the subject, understanding, and persuasion/presentation skills.

You must appreciate that success in this subject requires acceptable performance across all five competencies – you cannot trade off superb achievement in one against poor accomplishment in another, except in very minor ways that are unlikely to affect the final outcome.

As you embark on your study programme leading to the examinations, it's a good idea to assess yourself rigorously (along a 10-point scale, with zero indicating 'complete ignorance or inadequacy', and 10 implying complete command of the subject-matter or the competency in question) against all five 'BACKUP' competencies. If you are worried that your self-assessment may not be sufficiently objective, then of course it would be worthwhile to seek the opinions of others who know you well, and in particular your immediate manager or team leader.

The areas where you score low are those that require concentrated attention, and in undertaking your CPD activities throughout the study programme you should set yourself some learning goals for the 'BACKUP' competencies where effort is most needed. If you have a personal tutor you should tell them what you are doing, and why: it may well be that they can help you, by providing some additional ways in which the selected competencies can be acquired or developed, and by supplying you with appropriate feedback from your assignments, practice case studies and other written work undertaken throughout the study programme.

Another key point is that you must set yourself the personal goal of attaining an examination mark of at least 60 per cent. Merely aiming for a Pass (50 per cent) is too dangerous: as Chief Examiner I suspect that many candidates who were 'satisficing', ie doing just enough work to 'get by' with a mark of 50 per cent, eventually fail the examination because on the day they do not perform at their best, or because they find that the mix of questions does not enable them to shine, or because they fail to address the case study in a productive manner. Conversely, if you aim to achieve 60 per cent you have equipped yourself with a safety margin and, what's more, you will feel more confident when you enter the examination room, so your performance will automatically improve anyway.

Now let's look through the five 'BACKUP' competencies to see what is needed and how you can get there.

■ Competency 1: Business focus

This competency means that people are (actual or potential) value-added contributors to corporate purposes. The important question to ask about any employee is not 'What do you do?' but rather 'What are you for?', because strictly speaking nobody is employed to do anything – they are employed to achieve results and deliver outputs. This is why job descriptions are so dangerous if they encourage employees to believe that what matters is the extent to which the tasks listed in the job description are performed, when what really matters is the attainment of key accountabilities and the central 'mission' of any given role. To take an example, checkout operators in a supermarket perform a range of tasks, but these are subordinate to their central 'mission', which may be 'to ensure that the customer wants to come back'.

A *business focus* also means that existing processes and procedures have to be evaluated against the expectation that they will add value or at the very least that their benefits exceed their costs. Someone exhibiting *business focus* will frequently ask 'Why do we ...?' about current personnel/HR systems and conventional approaches, and 'Why don't we ...?' about the possibilities for reform, continuous improvement and change.

To develop your own capabilities in the *business focus* arena, here are some action-planning possibilities.

- Ask questions and collect information about the higher-order business purposes in your own organisation and also within your department or function.

- Bearing in mind that by making a commitment to the PDS programme you have also made a commitment to career professionalism across sectors other than the one in which you happen to be currently employed, collect all the literature and materials you can find about the links between people resourcing and *business focus* in other organisations. If you work in the public sector, make a special point of learning about the private sector, and vice versa.

- Specifically seek out information from academic research that is relevant to this subject, such as the recent studies by Professor John Purcell of the University of Bath (published by the CIPD in May 2003, and featured in a number of *People Management* articles – see the issue dated 15 May 2003). Purcell's investigations have concentrated on the importance of what he calls the 'big idea' as a unifying force in the best-performing organisations.

- If you have Internet access, consult the search engines to learn what you can about organisations which have 'world-class' reputations both for results and for people effectiveness, such as Singapore Airlines, Tesco, First Direct, Nokia and Microsoft (please note, however, that these are only examples – there are plenty of others, which are not necessarily household names but which nonetheless have managed to achieve impressive levels of integration between people commitment and organisational goals).

- It's a good idea, too, to work collaboratively with others – perhaps colleagues in your study programme – to assemble and share information. If your study programme involves attendance at a college or university, it is likely that some of your fellow students will be employed by organisations where *business focus* among people (and among HR professionals) is well established, and you can learn from them – just as you can share your experience and knowledge with them. Here it's worth pointing out that passing the CIPD examinations is not a competitive exercise. Theoretically everyone could be successful, provided they met the CIPD professional standards. So, if you spread the study load by co-operating with others, you can all benefit and nobody is disadvantaged.

■ Competency 2: Application capability

Application capability refers to the talent for designing and presenting practical, cost-effective and business-relevant solutions to problems, plus decisive, innovative and imaginative actions for addressing opportunities. It is a competency that is tested principally through the case study – almost always you will be invited to produce recommendations as if to a senior executive or the chief executive officer – but it may also be relevant to some of the issues raised in Section B. For instance, the May 2003 People Resourcing paper included a question in which candidates were required to construct 'practical steps' that an organisation could take in order to address the 'problem' of retaining and promoting women.

Whatever recommendations you produce, they will be well received by the examiners if they are (a) directly and convincingly linked to the 'problem' you are trying to solve or the 'opportunity' you are trying to seize; (b) sufficiently detailed to enable the examiners to be persuaded that you know what you are writing about; and (c) accompanied by an authoritative rationale or cost-benefit calculation to show how implementing what you propose will lead to consequences that are advantageous not just to the organisation's employees but also to its overall performance (measured in terms of profitability, customer satisfaction or other credible factors).

By contrast, here are some examples of recommendations that were advanced by various candidates who entered the Employee Resourcing examination in November 2002 and whose case study responses included the following: 'Implement a good appraisal system', 'Introduce motivation themes', 'Ensure the correct training and development has taken place', and 'Implement management performance initiatives'. As the Chief Examiner wrote at the time, how are we expected to know what a 'good appraisal system' looks like? What does it mean to 'introduce motivation themes'? Where do 'correct' training and development begin and end?

Another point is that even when students say the right thing (ie produce statements that reflect the CIPD's values and the strategic vision of the thinking performer for the PDS), they will get no credit for doing so if their statements appear to be made up of nothing more than platitudinous rhetoric. Here is an example, again taken from the Employee Resourcing cohort in November 2002: 'The right people with the right skills required to add value and competitive advantage to the company. In today's turbulent, highly competitive market, flexible, innovative, high-performing employees are required. Thinking performers are the way forward.' This treatment manages to encapsulate virtually every high-sounding cliché in the current personnel/HR arena, yet it says nothing convincing or credible in terms of application.

To develop your skills along the *application capability* continuum, you should be undertaking the following development initiatives.

- Especially if your current role does not require you ever to generate action proposals and recommendations, it is a good idea to consult with your manager, explain your need to acquire *application capability* credentials, and seek his/her co-operation in giving you a small-scale situation to investigate – perhaps the current car parking arrangements, or the design of your job descriptions, or the layout of the Personnel/HR Department's reception area – so that you can practise your skills at generating credible routes for problem-solving and continuous improvement. In addition, producing a short project analysis about the situation you have investigated will help you with report-writing techniques. What you must do is take note of any feedback about the recommendations you produce and then implement the feedback with a second practice exercise.

- In preparing for the People Resourcing examination, it is essential that you undertake some rehearsal activities, so far as the case study is concerned, by attempting some past case studies and then reviewing your work against the Chief Examiner's commentary included in his report on the examination results.

- Whenever you have produced some recommendations for dealing with a given situation (whether a case study or a 'real life' scenario), leave your work for 24 hours and then look at your proposals again. Ask yourself whether they are sufficiently precise, specific and informative to enable the imagined addressee to act on them as they stand; if they are not, then supply the necessary extra details. To say that an organisation needs 'a performance management system' is not helpful; to suggest that it should introduce a performance management system specifically targeted towards the Customer Services function, with targets focused on customer satisfaction, customer retention and customer referral, is much more authoritative.

- One very useful way to promote a sensible approach to the construction of meaningful recommendations, if you are part of a study programme with some fellow students, is to create a number of syndicate groups in order to address a typical case study, and then require each group to present its analysis and proposals to the rest of the cohort – simultaneously making it clear that all suggestions for change or improvement must be challenged if ambiguous or seemingly unrelated to business purposes. Exposing yourself and your colleagues to peer review can be a powerful mechanism for performance development.

Competency 3: Knowledge of the subject

The Chief Examiner always recommends that students should be thoroughly familiar with about 50 per cent of the Indicative Content, and adequately familiar with the rest. The structure of the PDS examinations – a case study followed by a choice of seven from ten shorter questions in Section B – makes the ancient art of 'question-spotting' much more difficult, if not impossible, and that, of course, is one of the principal reasons the examination has that particular structure, because we want the examination to be a genuine test of student capability.

So candidates must become at least moderately acquainted with every topic from the Indicative Content. That means, too, that students must keep up to date, because it is entirely legitimate for the Chief Examiner to introduce question topics that may not have been mentioned directly in the Indicative Content but which have become 'hot' issues within the people resourcing field. In recent examinations, questions have been asked about emotional intelligence, the so-called 'war for talent', and employer branding, even though none of these appeared in the 'syllabus'.

To acquire the expected degree of breadth of subject-matter knowledge, you should be taking these actions.

- At the commencement of your study programme, it is necessary to purchase a concertina file with about 20 separate compartments, and then give labels to each compartment derived from the principal areas of the Indicative Content, such as 'HR Planning', 'Special Case Scenarios' and so forth. As your study unfolds, you should assiduously assemble materials from whatever sources are available to you – copies of *People Management*, other HR or business periodicals (especially those available in your work location and/or reception area), items downloaded from the Internet, public-domain documents from your own organisation and from others (eg recruitment literature, competency frameworks or performance-appraisal system briefing notes), cuttings from the quality press, etc. Again, if you are attending a study programme in a college or university, you should set up a co-operative data-collection system with colleagues so that the productivity of your collective experience is maximised. Thus, if the class meets once weekly, everybody brings one item per week, with sufficient copies to enable the group to have one each; if tutors can be actively involved in this process, then so much the better.

- You must purchase a core textbook, either *People Resourcing* by Stephen Taylor (CIPD) or *Employment Resourcing* by Corbridge and Pilbeam (FT Publishing). Having obtained the book, it is then necessary to initiate a planned sequence of 'active reading' sessions to enable key parts of the text to be learned, because unfortunately the knowledge in the book will not transmit itself into your brain without your making a conscious effort to help the process along. In my view, 'active reading' sessions should not last for longer than an hour at a time, otherwise your concentration starts to wander, but you should schedule at least three such 'active reading' slots each week. For 'active reading' purposes, you must identify a quiet location, or wear ear-plugs if necessary, and remove all distractions, which may mean that you should sit at a table or a desk facing a featureless wall (don't sit where you can look out of the window, otherwise you may find things going on out there that will distract you from your purpose). Having chosen a key chapter, 'active reading' requires that you make notes, highlight quotations, underline key points, and in short do everything you can to guarantee that (a) you concentrate totally on the words in front of you, and (b) the information it contains enters your brain and remains there. After each 'active reading' hour, reward yourself with a small treat.

- In the period immediately prior to the examination, when you are revising, a key part of your revision activity must be a diligent review of the materials in your concertina file and the notes you made within each of your 'active reading' periods. It is advisable once more to use 'active reading' techniques at this point in your studies, too, ie underlining, highlighting, taking notes, and even reading aloud if you find it helps in the memory-retention process.

■ Competency 4: Understanding

The CIPD examinations are not so much a test of knowledge, but more a test of attitude and critical awareness. Rarely are any questions posed that call for nothing more than the reproduction of previously ingested information – almost always, students are invited first to describe, but then to explain, to evaluate, to analyse, to assess. This is why it is so healthy for candidates to adopt a permanently questioning mentality (even if such a mentality is not always welcomed when displayed in the work environment); and, of course, such a mentality is appropriate in a professional context because of the general expectation that personnel/HR practitioners must continue to innovate and to challenge.

Possession of a critical understanding, too, is a requirement of the PDS, given that it is a postgraduate qualification that is subject to what are known as the 'M level' descriptors, namely, that students must display:

- a systematic understanding of knowledge and a critical awareness of current problems and/or new insights

- a comprehensive understanding of techniques

- originality in the application of knowledge

- a conceptual understanding that enables both current research and methodologies to be evaluated critically

- the ability to deal with complex issues both systematically and creatively, make sound judgments in the absence of complete data, and communicate conclusions

- the demonstration of self-direction and originality in tackling and solving problems, plus the willingness to act autonomously in planning and implementing tasks

- a continued drive to advance knowledge, understanding and skills (principally through CPD).

So here are some ways in which *understanding* can be acquired and developed within a study programme leading to the CIPD examinations:

- Undertaking the 'active reading' sessions, as outlined above, should enable you to assimilate some of the required mentality, since it is demonstrated at length in both of the textbooks identified by name.

- Critical faculties are enhanced when individuals learn to seek authoritative evidence for statements and apparently factual propositions that may reflect nothing more than conventional wisdom. For instance, it is commonly believed that one-to-one selection interviews present opportunities for psychological prejudice, the 'halo effect' and subjective judgements, yet these phenomena are absent, or relatively absent, from the panel interview. Equally, it may be argued that if two or three people are involved in candidate selection, either as panel members or in a sequence of one-to-one interviews, then multiplicity of numbers moves the final decision nearer to absolute objectivity. There is not a shred of evidence to support either of these conclusions. Lots of evidence, on the other hand, exists to show that the traditional selection interview has a very low predictive validity, yet many interviewers regard themselves as exceptions to this general rule, and will reject the evidence or even pretend that it does not exist. The budding personnel/HR professional must cope with these (sometimes emotive) issues, but must continue to challenge, to search for worthwhile evidence, and to promote a dispassionate approach to the creation of action-planning options.

- In addressing examination questions where it is appropriate for third-party sources of evidence and research to be cited, it is now, more than ever, important for CIPD students to incorporate such references into their answer treatments. It is not enough simply to write, 'Research has indicated that …' ; instead, candidates must be able to point out that 'Research by Marcus Buckingham, reported in *People Management* (October 2001), concludes that only about 17 per cent of employees are genuinely "engaged" in their work and within their organisations.'

■ Competency 5: Persuasion and presentation skills

It is true that relatively little attention is paid by the examiners to the presentation of answers within Section B, especially as students have relatively little time in which to consider the technicalities of layout and design if they have to produce seven answers within an hour. Even so, it has to be admitted that material that is 'reader-friendly' does convey a better impression than pages that are difficult to decipher, disorganised and incoherent. With Section A, the case study, this is even more important, because characteristically candidates are required to produce their responses in the form of a report addressed to, say, the chief executive or the HR director, so some adherence to the canons of businesslike report-writing is expected. (On the other hand, there is no guarantee that every case study scenario will require the answer to be produced as a report: in the recent past, candidates have been asked for 'action guidelines' to be presented to franchise-holders for a chain of beauty and body therapy shops, and detailed 'briefing notes' for the recruitment and selection of customer-service assistants at petrol stations. Unfortunately, some individuals, evidently well trained in report-writing, persist in producing reports even when specifically required not to do so, and lose marks accordingly for their refusal to adhere to instructions.]

If a report is requested, then candidates should adhere broadly speaking to the following presentational criteria:

- Begin with a title page, having selected a title that summarises what the report is supposed to be about, ie its purposes (rather than its content).

- An outline contents page should follow, though in the context of an examination the page numbers are likely to be fictional rather than authentic. At least the contents summary should give an indication of the report structure, with section or chapter titles, especially embracing 'Conclusions' and 'Recommendations' (these must be treated separately and not amalgamated).

- It is desirable, though not compulsory, to produce a short, one-paragraph 'Summary' of the report as a whole, not just its recommendations.

- Usually, the section/chapter titles will begin with an 'Introduction' and possibly a 'Method of Investigation' paragraph, followed by 'Findings'. However, the word 'Findings' should not be used: it is far preferable to select titles that are more closely linked to the subject-matter.

- Within each section, material should be organised in short paragraphs and/or sub-paragraphs, numbered sequentially, with some cross-referencing where appropriate. It is definitely not appropriate to develop the text as if writing an essay, since it then becomes more difficult for the busy reader to disentangle analysis from description, and inference from recommendation.

- Recommendations should be as detailed and specific as possible, preferably prioritised, and accompanied by a brief cost-benefit evaluation. If the case study brief has called for separate questions to be answered, then the material in the report should be similarly separated.

- There are certain verbal and phrase formulations that are to be avoided, especially in the Recommendations. If the word 'hopefully' is used, it implies that the author is uncertain about either the recommendation itself or its consequences – and this is no way to convince the imagined reader that the proposal is likely to work. Equally undesirable is 'I feel', 'I would suggest' and similar variants, as the executive to whom the report is addressed should not be interested in the author's 'feelings' but rather in the degree of dispassionate situational analysis that has been undertaken.

- It is far preferable, therefore, for students to adopt a confident, assertive style for both the Recommendations and also the content of answers generally. Proposals for action can be much more authoritative if they are reinforced by meaningful research references or by the citation of other corporate instances where similar ideas have already been implemented with conspicuous success.

Pre-examination practice with report-writing and indeed with examination techniques as a whole is an essential part of the study programme. Initially, I recommend that you address one or two past People/Employee Resourcing case studies but do so without feeling the need to adhere to strict time limits, since the important skill to develop is proficiency in situational analysis, problem-solving and continuous improvement.

■ Some final thoughts

In 1993, the Personnel Standards Lead Body commissioned some research in an effort to discover what chief executives thought about the personnel/HR function and its typical practitioners. The research identified some negative perceptions which, I am afraid, still exist (with justification) in certain quarters and in certain organisations:

- Some personnel/HR professionals seem to think more about the exercise of their professional skills than about the extent to which they could make a positive strategic and operational contribution to the organisation by which they are employed.

- Many demonstrate an over-conscious concern for rules, procedures and employment law, to the point where they appear to take a positive delight in raising objections to proposed managerial initiatives rather than in facilitating the translation of such initiatives into tangible outcomes.

- HR/personnel professionals are often enthusiastic about introducing systems and procedures that fail because they are not sufficiently tailored to meet the needs of the business and also because they are not owned by management.

- In many enterprises, the function adopts an indiscriminate approach to being a 'good employer', unrelated to, say, the precise circumstances of the labour market in a given environment and the resources available to the organisation.

Even if some of these criticisms are founded on mistaken stereotypes as opposed to hard evidence, it is imperative to undermine such impressions where they continue – and consistent adoption of the thinking performer perspective and a contributor culture will both contribute to the attainment of a new vision. Here are some key mistakes often made by students when they implicitly portray an isolationist, insular, 'professional' perspective uninformed by any genuine concern for the real world and the corporate context:

- Proposing recommendations for action that say nothing about costs and nothing about the business benefits.

- Where benefits are outlined, assessing them solely against 'professional' criteria.

- Adoption of an assumed paradigm of 'best practice' without regard for organisational realities. Although the term 'good practice' is acceptable, 'best practice' suggests an idealistic, utopian state of affairs to which all enterprises should aspire, and a scenario that therefore militates against innovation.

Indeed, 'best practice' often refers to nothing more than adherence to a systematic recruitment/selection model – HR planning, job analysis, job descriptions, person specifications, and so forth – which is not the framework conventionally adopted by 'world-class' companies.

- The implication that the personnel/HR function is a self-contained entity rather than a positive contributor to the fulfilment of a strategic vision and the organisation's competitive advantage in its wider market place.

Getting it right, by contrast, involves these key considerations – which apply not just within the PDS examinations but also in the practical realities of career success:

- Answers in the examination must emphasise a close degree of integration between people management, the HR/personnel function, and the imperatives of the 'business' (whether in the private sector or elsewhere, since increasingly public-sector organisations are measured against private-sector priorities).

- Equally, answers must demonstrate a genuine concern about meeting the requirements of the 'customers' who ultimately pay for the presence of people resourcing professionals and whose opinions therefore count (or should count) for a great deal. (When the Chief Examiner asked a short question recently in which students were invited to indicate the 'customers' for people resourcing, many wrote about job applicants and other 'stakeholders', but few considered it relevant to suggest that perhaps the proper role for people resourcing professionals is to create and administer recruitment and selection systems that make it easier for the organisation's board of directors to achieve their stated strategic and aspirational goals for the enterprise. Thus, if the business has decided to make customer service its competitive advantage, and wants this focus to form part of every employee's toolkit, then customer service must be written into job descriptions and accountability profiles, become part of person specifications and competency frameworks, and form a key dimension of the recruitment and selection system in the way it treats applicants.)

- When formulating recommendations, especially within the case study, candidates should acknowledge the likelihood that at least some of their proposals will have to encounter implementation barriers. These should be mentioned and a brief account given of the ways in which such barriers could be overcome or minimised in practice.

- Linked to this same argument is the fact that CIPD students (no matter how young and innocent) need to demonstrate their awareness of the 'political' realities of organisational life. In many instances from the recent past, where a Section A case study has specified that the answer is to be written in the form of a report for the chief executive officer, individuals have included in their recommendations the statement that the chief executive officer should be dismissed or coerced into early retirement. Such suggestions are frequently unwise; if the departure of the chief executive officer is desirable (as it sometimes is), then this is a course of action that has to be presented with tact and sensitivity, often with a dignified escape route provided.

- Examination answers should contain fewer references to 'professionalism' and 'best practice', but more about 'business benefits', 'continuous improvement', 'competitive advantage' and 'cross-sector benchmarking'.

- One further key factor which candidates would do very well to bear in mind is that the Chief Examiner can only judge what appears in the answer book, because he has no other information available to him about the student's state of mind, the amount of information residing in the student's brain (though not reproduced in the answer book), and what the student might have said had more time been available. This means that *candidates must sell themselves as vigorously as possible*: knowledge, understanding and other capabilities can only be assessed by the extent to which they have been demonstrated explicitly. Relatively few individuals make it clear that they have read any source materials, not even the CIPD textbook; relatively few mention their own work experiences; few cite any third-party sources of evidence or research, or any benchmark applications of 'good practice' in the field of People Resourcing. Students who behave in this fashion are making it more difficult for themselves, because in the 'shop window' of the answer book they have deliberately chosen to turn the lighting off and keep their 'goods' under wraps.

There are some specific issues with regard to examination technique, moreover. There are significant numbers of candidates who begin by addressing Section B (seven questions within an hour), write at excessive length on some topics, and then leave themselves with insufficient time to do justice to the case study. It is more sensible to devote the pre-examination reading time to a thorough scrutiny of the case study brief and then, when writing commences, make some notes before embarking on the answer itself, especially as the majority of Section B questions, though requiring thought, are typically more straightforward and can be tackled without so much cerebral preparation. It is also important to remember that the two halves of the examination are meant to complement each other, especially as they confront differing competencies, and the examiner does not allow an excellent result for Section B to compensate for inadequate achievement in Section A, or vice versa.

Conscientious and efficient management of the available time has to be an important skill for the CIPD examinations. For this reason alone, some pre-examination practice will pay dividends, but there are other considerations as well. These days, very few people use handwriting at work or anywhere else – they are much more likely to operate a keyboard – yet until we can guarantee the universal availability of word processors in examination centres, we have to require CIPD candidates to produce their answers in long-hand. This process can be physically exhausting, particularly for individuals unaccustomed to such activity, and practice to build up the necessary muscles would be time well spent.

Bearing in mind the performance criteria expected from a thinking performer, then a 'good' Section B answer will generally include elements of knowledge display, critical evaluation, third-party referencing (from relevant research or literature, such as the textbook), and an attempt to link the question theme to the student's own work experience or to a named organisational scenario. Of course, not all Section B topics lend themselves to this somewhat simplistic model, but most do and this should be the prescription adopted.

Last but very definitely not least, it is essential to answer the question. When estate agents are asked about the top three factors that determine the price and value of a piece of property, they usually reply, 'Location, location, location'. Similarly, answering the question needs to be emphasised three times: answer the question, answer the question, answer the question. Marks will not be given for content, however well-informed, if it is unrelated to the central issues, and marks will not be given for superfluous material, like words of greeting or farewell. Section B of the PDS examination for People Resourcing is structured round ten e-mail messages, and candidates must select seven, showing how they would respond. Despite the fact that the rubric for the examination paper clearly states what is expected ('You are required to indicate the content of your proposed response'), some have found it necessary to produce entirely gratuitous remarks, such as 'Sorry for the delay in replying, I have just got back from a meeting' or 'Hi, sorry, I meant to come and talk to you about this'.

■ Conclusion

In preparing for the examination there are many points to consider and many guidelines to follow, but perhaps unfortunately there are no quick and easy routes to success (if there were, they would have been discovered by now). However, if you act on the advice contained in these notes, you will deserve to succeed and you will undoubtedly do so, and the lessons learned will be invaluable to you throughout your subsequent career.

• GUIDANCE TO CANDIDATES FROM THE CIPD EXAMINER

Within the framework already described earlier in this Revision Guide, the Chief Examiner has specified the following detailed ingredients as the basis for assessing student performance:

Positive

- Demonstrates *business focus* through a good understanding of HR/corporate strategy

- Appears sensitive to wider 'political' and organisational issues

- Equipped with *application capability*, generating recommendations that are cogent, specific and convincing

- At least some recommendations show evidence of original and innovative thinking

- Confronts implementation problems – in other words, shows how 'big picture' recommendations could be translated into operational and tangible actions

- Shows thorough *knowledge of the relevant subject-matter*

- Reinforces knowledge with *critical understanding* – challenges conventional wisdom and current practices

- Adequate inclusion of references to third-party sources, such as relevant literature, research evidence and so forth

- Draws on appropriate organisational examples to show good practice or world-class benchmarking possibilities and potential

- Makes use of own work experience scenarios in analytical fashion, going beyond mere description

- Answers are well-presented and persuasive, lucid and articulate, especially the case study.

Negative

- Absence of *business orientation* – appears to be driven by 'professional' priorities and abstract, indiscriminate personnel/HR imperatives

- No coherent *application capability* – relies on general, undeveloped platitudes unrelated to the task in hand

- Knowledge of the subject-matter poor, demonstrating a mixture of ignorance and significant factual mistakes

- No evidence of *critical understanding*, with answers largely confined to superficial description and low-level analysis

- Few or no references to relevant third-party evidence and/or organisational examples (not even the core textbook)

- *Persuasion and presentation* poor, with arguments difficult to follow, material hard to read, unelaborated bullet points, lack of co-ordination between 'Findings', 'Conclusions' and 'Recommendations'

- Answers typically too discursive, betraying lack of focus on the key issues to be addressed.

The results from the May 2003 entry indicate that there is some way to go before the performance expectations associated with the PDS will be fully absorbed, particularly so far as critical understanding and the thinking performer paradigm are concerned. In what follows I have summarised the key issues, initially for the examination as a whole, then for each section, and ultimately for the specific questions themselves.

The key issues: The examination as a whole

The Chief Examiner and his colleagues in the marking team rigorously applied the '2+10+5' assessment criteria to each script (see Preface). It was also seen as important to view each candidate's script with the postgraduate or 'M' level requirements in mind. Thus any statements of 'fact' should have been reinforced by citations from appropriate third-party sources, and there should be evidence of the willingness to challenge conventional wisdom or even research findings (not all research findings are factual merely because they have resulted from research – in many cases the methodologies may be flawed, the samples unrepresentative, and the analysis characterised by wishful thinking). Candidates were also expected to exhibit a well-informed understanding of the practice of personnel/HR outside their immediate organisational and business sector, and should not have been narrowly focused on ethical/legal compliance as the ultimate measure of HR performance.

Against these criteria, the following considerations deserve your attention (given that you are presumably reading this as a future examination candidate for People Resourcing):

1   A significant proportion of scripts continue to contain no references whatsoever to any sources of evidence, research, a textbook or third-party material of any kind. From the evidence, therefore, the Chief Examiner would be entitled to conclude that such students had undertaken no reading, little preparation, and had certainly not taken advantage of, say, Stephen Taylor's excellent CIPD-published book. Since the inclusion of citations from external sources is now a critical feature of PDS expectations, then students who do not incorporate such material in their scripts must stand little chance of success.

2   It is not enough simply to produce vague phrases like 'Research indicates …' or 'Research suggests …' or even 'Research from various sources suggests …' Although citations from such populist periodicals as *Personnel Today* are better than nothing, they are still not taking the issue of evidence-based argument far enough.

3   Occasionally candidates continue to harm their chances of success by excelling in one part of the examination while performing disastrously in the other. The CIPD rules clearly state that anyone will fail if they are awarded fewer than 40 per cent of the available marks in either section (this rule was deliberately created in order to ensure that a comprehensive range of competencies is tested).

■ The key issues: Section A

The case study treatment was marked out of 100, with up to 50 marks for each of the two specific questions posed. There was no specific mark allocation for presentation quality, ie the organisation of the answer material into a structured report (as specified in the brief), but this element was taken into account when awarding marks more generally. It was expected that in the first question – about the difficulties of culture change – students would concentrate on the people resourcing aspects, ie new specifications about the role for people, new types of recruitment and selection techniques, new approaches to motivation, leadership and performance management, and so forth. If examples of relevant culture change were to be used to reinforce this part of the answer treatment, they could have been found in organisations that have decided to outsource their back-office functions to a specialist provider, possibly operating overseas, or in those which have replaced full-time, long-serving staff by fixed-term contractual employees, or in companies that have moved from centralised paternalism to devolved empowerment (eg Sainsburys).

As far as the second question was concerned, there were 50 marks available for the answer as a whole, which needed to address all three specified themes, namely, the proposed competency framework for the 'consultant' role, the selection methods to be used, and the action to be taken in the case of existing supervisors who either did not want to be, or lacked the capabilities of becoming, 'consultants' themselves. Anyone failing to cover any one of the three themes automatically sacrificed approximately 15 marks; further marks could have been lost if individuals ignored the requirement that recommendations should be reinforced by references to appropriate research material and benchmarking evidence from other organisations.

In practice, some of the key learning points for future students will have to be derived from these observations:

1 Despite the fact that the 'terms of reference' was clearly divided into two separate topic areas, some answers did not conform to this obligation – and so dividing the 'report' into its component parts merely added gratuitously to the Chief Examiner's task.

2 As the Professional Qualification Scheme has evolved incrementally (but also transformationally) into the Professional Development Scheme, one constant feature has remained, namely, the virtual inevitability of the fact that case study answers should be structured as a report. A significant proportion of candidates continue to ignore this requirement: they produce no title page, no contents page, no introduction, no clearly delineated recommendations, no distinction between 'findings' and 'conclusions'.

3 In terms of writing style, too, many do not organise their text into numbered paragraphs and sub-paragraphs, but prefer to present their thoughts as an undifferentiated stream of consciousness, facts mixed up with interpretation, conclusions mixed up with recommendations, and topics addressed haphazardly throughout. (This difficulty can easily be resolved if a 'rough plan' is produced before the answer proper is written.) Paragraphs can easily become over-long (a page or so), and the resultant material is very definitely not reader-friendly.

4 The Chief Examiner in the past has criticised the apparent reluctance of many candidates to generate assertive, decisive and confident proposals for action, but unfortunately this continues to be a difficulty. Two examples (from separate scripts) will suffice: 'Look at the possibility of consultants with expertise in change management to help introduce as smoothly as possible,' and 'It may be a good idea to run an assessment centre.' As you are reading this, imagine what your reactions would be if you had commissioned this report and the author had presented you with recommendations as weak, hesitant and indecisive as these – and then ask yourself how the recommendations could be changed to make them more acceptable. It's not difficult, is it?

5 The two tasks were to be undertaken as a service to the chief executive of your company, Dr Tomkinson, who wishes to introduce an IMS-type culture into his own business. Task 1 asked for a review of the problems associated with a shift of people-resourcing philosophies, plus some evidence-based proposals about how to make the changes easier to accomplish and assimilate; task 2 sought advice about the methods of implementing the new philosophy. It was surprising and disappointing, therefore, that so many individuals devoted much of their available time and space to what can only be described as an exercise in negativity. For them, the problems were enormous and virtually insuperable, and the provision of constructive help, plus a 'can-do' attitude, was noticeably absent. Future students would do well to remember that if they are to add value in their organisations, it is their principal role to assist in the furtherance of stated corporate goals, and although it is legitimate to articulate concerns about the difficulties, it is not appropriate to dwell on them indefinitely.

6   More specifically, the obligation to produce a competency framework for the new 'consultant' role was a cause of many difficulties – even though several case studies in the PQS Employee Resourcing examination have also focused on competencies, many organisations currently use competency frameworks (instead of person specifications), and there has been extensive literature about competencies, published by the CIPD and in *People Management*. If a competency-based approach is to work, then each competency has to be defined in some detail, and so vague (unelaborated) titles like 'Understanding', 'Knowledge' and 'Diversity' are totally inadequate. Several scripts simply offered a list of so-called competencies without any supporting explanation or rationale at all; and a significant minority avoided the issue altogether, claiming instead that 'A competency framework must be put together', but omitting to indicate what it could comprise.

7   The 'terms of reference' sought evidence-based proposals (because this is now part of the performance expectation associated with the PDS, although of course proposals derived from evidence should be a normal aspect of any advocacy advanced by a properly performing personnel/HR practitioner anyway). This is a requirement that a large number of examination candidates have yet to take seriously. Instead, many recommendations were advanced as if the case for their implementation was self-evident, eg the use of assessment centres, psychometric testing, work practice tests, 'tandem interviews with 2–3 people present to give a more objective view', emotional intelligence capability evaluation, etc. Frankly, such a cavalier approach will not in future be acceptable. If the use of assessment centres is being promoted or defended, then students must seek to show how the costs involved (particularly as they are considerable) can be justified against the potential benefits of improved predictive validity in the selection process; glib references to 'psychometric testing' must be reinforced with an indication of their scope and scale; work practice tests must be accompanied by a brief acknowledgement of the research evidence about their usefulness; the assumption that interviews involving two or three people are somehow 'more objective' should be vigorously challenged; and the fashionable enthusiasm for emotional intelligence has to be tempered by some notes of analytical caution.

■ The key issues: Section B

For People Resourcing, the Section B questions are presented as a collection of e-mail messages for which suitable responses must be devised. Although there are significant time constraints, given the need to produce seven answers in the space of about 60 minutes, candidates are nonetheless expected to adhere to the general '2+10+5' requirements across the examination as a whole. In principle, a competent Section B treatment will contain elements of description (addressing knowledge of the subject-matter), critical evaluation and commentary, third-party referencing of relevant literature and research sources, and application examples from the candidate's own work experience or from (preferably named) other organisations. Not all Section B questions lend themselves to this recipe design, yet nonetheless it is a formula that should be borne in mind both within the examination and also during all pre-examination rehearsals.

From an administrative point of view, each Section B answer is marked out of 20, with a formal allocation of marks within that figure for questions that have two or three parts (this ensures that if students fail to address any sub-question, they automatically sacrifice a proportion of the marks available).

A review of the entries for May 2003 has revealed the following learning points for future candidates:

1   Just as estate agents say, 'Location, location, location' when invited to list the top three factors which determine the value of a property, so the Chief Examiner has to reiterate the point that 'Answer the question, answer the question, answer the question' are the top three factors which determine the mark awarded. The new PDS provides an opportunity for choosing questions (given that candidates must select seven from the ten available), yet even so there are too many instances where individuals do not directly confront the topic but write about something else instead. It may be argued that they have genuinely misunderstood what is required, but this is unlikely, especially in view of the detailed and meticulous question-review process undertaken by the CIPD in collaboration with its Chief Examiners before the examination paper is finally agreed. Question 4 asked about the desirability of recruiting extraverts for call-centre roles; some evaded this point altogether but confined themselves to lengthy advice about the selection techniques that should be used; Question 1 focused on the benefits and hazards of rating scales, but several wrote instead about the benefits and hazards of performance appraisal.

2   Although the general background setting for Section B was the arrival of ten e-mail messages, it was not necessary to structure any answers as if they were themselves e-mail messages; indeed, the rubric specifically indicated that 'You are required to indicate the content of your proposed response; the method through which you transmit your response (by e-mail, face-to-face discussion, etc) need not be specified.' Nonetheless, a significant proportion of entrants to the examination wasted valuable seconds by writing entirely gratuitous greetings ('Hi, sorry for the delay in replying, I have just got back from a meeting', or 'Hi, sorry, I meant to come and talk to you about this') for which no marks were available. An even more unnecessary instance of time-wasting is this opening sentence for a treatment to Question 6 (about the new employment rights that came into effect in April 2003): 'Thank you for your recent e-mail regarding the new employment rights that have come into effect on 6 April 2003. Identified below are the two main rights that I think will effect [sic] your organisation the most.' It is essential for students to concentrate solely on making written statements that could conceivably earn marks – superfluous greetings and vacuous introductory comments cannot do so. Nor is it necessary for simplistic definitions to be supplied for the words and phrases used in a question (in tackling Question 2, about the predictive validity of the selection interview, more than one person found it necessary to define the meaning of the term 'interview' – it is 'when a potential applicant is asked questions by one member or a number of members of staff').

As with Section A, many responses are supplied without any reinforcing evidence from third-party sources – indeed, as the Chief Examiner has pointed out in a sequence of reports on the results of the PQS Employee Resourcing examinations, it is not apparent from many scripts that the students concerned have consulted any relevant literature or research at all, not even the CIPD textbook by Stephen Taylor. It is vital that future candidates learn the simple techniques of referencing and citation – even a straightforward acknowledgment of some third-party source will be sufficient, and much better than nothing at all.

3 The tangible existence of complacency and corporate introspection continues to be widespread. One instance will suffice. In addressing Question 2, about the poor predictive validity associated with selection interviewing, candidates were asked to explain the continued popularity of the interview in their own organisations. One wrote: 'We continue to use it because it suits our organisational needs, it's cost-effective and our organisation is still very competitive and performance levels are maintained.' Leaving aside for a moment that the term 'cost-effective' has been used when the individual clearly means 'low cost', there is no 'thinking performer' attitude at work here, no recognition of the possibility that even if existing practices 'work' (whatever that might mean), they might nonetheless 'work' even better if their validity and reliability were properly evaluated. The prevalence of wishful thinking is widespread in organisations, of course, but that is no justification for its continued popularity among CIPD students.

4 At the same time, many of the scripts betrayed indications of genuine acceptance for the new performance expectations associated with the Professional Development Scheme, and the Chief Examiner is optimistic that the overall pass rate for People Resourcing will match expectations. Some questions in particular elicited very competent responses, particularly Question 4 (on whether extraverts are right for call centres), Question 5 (on e-recruitment), Question 6 (on new employment rights), and Question 9 (on the possible existence of a 'war for talent').

In conclusion, the Chief Examiner believes that no entirely new problems about student performance have come into existence as the Professional Development Scheme gets under way. Criticisms about the absence of third-party evidence, citation of independent sources, and referencing of research and literature, are criticisms that have been made in the past: the only difference is that such expectations are now more vigorously and explicitly required, and failure to comply with them is likely lead to a Fail outcome in the examination. Equally, criticisms about complacency, uninformed stereotyping about the practice of personnel/HR in business sectors with which the student is unfamiliar, and the failure to portray a 'thinking performer' attitude, are all considerations to which attention has been drawn in Chief Examiner reports about Employee Resourcing in the now-superseded Professional Qualification Scheme. Again, the only difference is that a 'thinking performer' perspective is absolutely crucial to assimilation of the CIPD's professional standards, so its absence now becomes a legitimate cause of a Fail outcome in the examination.

● THE CIPD's PEOPLE RESOURCING GENERALIST STANDARD

■ Introduction

To be able to function as a people resourcing (PR) professional it is clear that the individual must have a detailed understanding of the business in which they work and also the context in which their business operates, ie the social, political (legislative) and technological environments that affect what business does and how it can do it. Further, there is a need to consider systematically how we, as PR professionals, ply our trade. The CIPD Standards are designed to guide our thinking and actions with respect to the processes for which we are responsible.

The purpose of this chapter is to review the People Resourcing Generalist Standards in the context of the overall objectives of the CIPD thrust for development of a value-added contribution to business outcomes, and specifically with reference to the assessment of these Standards. The Standards are presented in headings below and in detail in Appendix 1 of this Revision Guide.

The *recommended text* for this elective is Stephen Taylor's *People Resourcing*, (2002, CIPD). Candidates working towards the examination can also find suggested further reading on the CIPD's website by going to the 'Home Page' and then follow the drop-down menus as detailed below:

Qualify Train → Qualifications → Professional Standards → Reading List

This provides a complete reading list to support all the Standards. The author has indicated further reading in the bibliography to this Revision Guide (page 90). The twice-monthly house journal of the Institute, *People Management*, is also vital reading.

Candidates will be expected to think through examination questions and apply good practice, making decisions and recommendations for action based upon informed opinion. This implies that, when preparing for the examination, candidates need to commit to memory examples of good practice, perhaps from *People Management*, Stephen Taylor's *People Resourcing* or from other recognised sources. Although candidates are not expected to quote verbatim research outcomes, they are expected to be aware of research and the commentators who have contributed to the field of research and its outcomes. They should also use references in support of, and to underpin, arguments or recommendations they may have when answering questions. For example, when discussing the reliability of selection techniques, candidates would be expected to give the relative reliabilities of the methodologies (Structured Interview, Assessment Centre etc, and indicate the source, eg Anderson and Shackleton or Smith *et al*).

The People Resourcing Standards

The CIPD Standards are presented under the following headings:

- Purpose
- Performance Indicators
  Operational Indicators
  Knowledge Indicators
- Indicative Content.

Purpose

This section, as well as contextualising the focus of the PR process, gives a clear direction as to what the human resources professional should be trying to achieve in his or her role as a business partner.

There has to be a marriage between operational transactional work and its outcomes and the added value element that can only be delivered by the thoughtful application of the knowledge and skills associated with the PR role.

Those entering the profession need both to focus on the 'here and now' as well as developing their understanding of the strategic way PR affects the business.

Performance Indicators

The *Performance Indicators* are considered in terms of what the HR practitioner must be able to do, and these are expressed as *Operational Indicators*. What the practitioner must be able to understand and explain are expressed as *Knowledge Indicators*.

The *Operational Indicators* cannot be assessed in the exam room because they are associated with the actual application of knowledge and skills in the workplace and so can only be assessed 'on the job'.

Indicative Content

The broad-brush *Operational* and *Knowledge Indicators* are given detailed meaning by the *Indicative Content*, of which there are ten sections:

1 People resourcing in context

2 The strategic significance of people resourcing

3 Approaches to people resourcing

4 Human resource planning

5 Recruitment and selection

6 People management

7 Special-case scenarios

8 Support tools for effective people resourcing

9 Compliance and ethicality in people resourcing

10 People resourcing: the future

■ Understanding the Performance Indicators

The development of the Performance Indicators is predicated upon developing staff who have the ability and motivation to meet the demands of the CIPD's concept of the *Thinking Performer*, which implies both personal challenge and reflection on how to:

- deliver better standards

- do things quicker and smarter

- reduce the costs of PR activities

– all while maintaining legal and regulatory compliance.

Accepting that 'I cannot make an impact in my organisation because I am not senior enough' is now considered thinking the unacceptable. We all have a contribution to make, and our ability to think and to demonstrate this quality will, given time, shake the foundations of the most backward-thinking organisations. Business, government, local government and other agencies cannot afford not to fully employ all their talent, at all levels.

Performance Indicators 1 and 2 have many things in common. They are about enhancing policies, processes and procedures. Individually we can continually challenge ourselves and test whether or not there is room for improvement. We should also consider the paradigms that corporately cause our organisation, and others, to reflect and to test what they, and we, do to challenge the status quo.

What are the examples from which I can quote? Maintaining a 'knitting vigilance' by monitoring *People Management*, *The Times* and similar quality broadsheets, the core and other recommended texts keeping abreast of research, especially work commissioned by the CIPD, contributes to informing opinion. The 'being aware of and appraised of issues' is part of the approach to business improvement. To complete the process there must be reflection, recommendation, debate and then action. Consider, for example, the whole paradigm of resourcing. Although the contingency approach to PR has been around since the 1950s, it has largely lain fallow until recently, and there is now a resurgence of interest. Academically, the contingency approach considers the best fit between process and the nature of the business. Large firms would have processes in place which reflect the need for uniformity of action, perhaps more bureaucracy, whereas the smaller firm, such as an advertising company, would see its differentiating characteristic, both in terms of how it sells itself to customers and also in how it attracts and retains staff, as 'being different'. The need to have well-tried policies and procedures is not seen as fitting with the company culture (Taylor, 2002:14). The essence of preparation, therefore, is to review and identify issues, to reflect upon them, ultimately leading to recommendations for action, or perhaps inaction. In the case quoted, the fact that the PR professional is aware of the trends should at least stimulate thought about whether or not the paradigm is relevant to his or her business.

1 Make constructive contributions to the development or enhancement of PR policies

Policies and procedures are specific to a subject area of the PR process but generic in terms of how we handle, create, review and revise them. No one chapter of Taylor's 2002 core text deals specifically with how policies should be handled. However, within each chapter he deals with good, bad and value-added practice. The clues about what we should be doing are there. The issue is, what are we doing about it? Is the good and especially valued-added practice included within the policies with which we work on a day-to-day basis?

The changing world in which we live and the technological advances in the integration of production methods and communications systems affect the way business operates within the UK and across borders. Political changes such as the fall of the Iron Curtain, the dropping of trade barriers with China and the latter's accession to the World Trade Organisation, and the 'aggrandisement' of the European Union have all increased the pace of change in how we work and the nature of the work. The fundamental relationship between employer and employee has changed, and the increasing influence of stakeholder interests are all reflected in the world in which we now work.

We are in a post-modern society (Huczynski and Buchanan 2001:58) where not only the technologies have changed but also societal and individual values.

Policies are in effect a plan of action and reflect the deliberations of and also capture the wisdom of those competent to make value judgements on sets of circumstances. The net result is a set of recommended actions in response to a set of circumstances. Circumstances, however, do change very quickly. Changes are brought about by macro- and micro-reasons, eg because of the destruction of the World Trade Center in New York in 2001 and its resulting impact upon the airline and tourism business with the reluctance of people to fly. Micro-changes caused by local competition in the labour market can all have a significant effect upon PR.

Processes need to be in place to review the relevance and efficacy of PR policies. It is about added value. Outdated and outmoded policies may be, at best, value-neutral and, at worst, cause frustration and not facilitate the business process.

The challenge has to be twofold. On the one hand, there is a continuous requirement to challenge the norm and to question and test what is in place against some form of yardstick. On the other, there has to be a pragmatism that reflects the limitations that are put on business processes because of resource constraints (manpower, cash or cashflow). It is a question of being able to understand these factors and being able to demonstrate that pragmatism of decision-making.

To give an example, the author was working in an overseas joint venture (JV) operation drilling for hydrocarbons in the North Caspian Sea. At one stage of the venture, before information that oil and gas had been found, circumstances were such that there was a clear requirement for additional competent staff to be able to adequately meet both the requirements of the drilling operation and the not-insubstantial reporting requirements of the JV shareholders. However, a business decision was taken to limit further recruitment because of the uncertainty of a positive outcome to the drilling operation. The well being drilled was a 'wildcat' (first well) in a 'prospect' that was being appraised for hydrocarbons. So until there was some indication that the well, and thus the prospect, was likely to produce hydrocarbons in economic quantities, further recruitment was restricted to the replacement only of key staff and people lost through attrition. Clearly, this was a painful decision but it was taken upon ethical and also practical considerations. Ethical, in the sense that the company wished to minimise the number of staff it would possibly have to make redundant should the well not produce hydrocarbons in commercial quantities, and practical in respect of the likely poor quality of staff who would apply for positions in a company with a possibly limited life-span. For management the issue was then to prepare for two scenarios:

1 a 'dry' well, with the consequent need to make staff redundant

2 a successful appraisal of the prospect and an immediate expansion of the project.

Scenario 1 implies a progressive scaling-down of operations.

Scenario 2 implies that the whole scale of the business changes, from a one-well JV operation, to a multi-billion dollar exploration and production programme. This sea change in activity would have to be reflected in new ways of doing business, new structures, strategies, policies etc. Clearly, time and effort were spent planning for this eventuality. Meantime the policy was communicated to staff as part of the open policy of sharing information.

• **Figure 1:** Delivering business objectives in a context of resource constraints

▶ **Source:** Taylor, 2002.

Reflecting upon the business practice of PR and sharing learning

Coming back to the matter in hand, how can the practitioner reflect in their work and in their professional studies and preparation for assessment this type of issue?

1 Firstly, this can be achieved by reflecting upon one's own business practice. How do you maintain a currency in policies and procedures within your work? Are they live working documents that truly reflect the needs of the business?

   • How are they audited?

   • What triggers cause (have caused) a revision of their relevance and effectiveness?

   • What are the strengths and weaknesses in current processes?

2   Secondly, what is good practice? Taylor (2002: ch15) gives some examples of how we can measure what we do in this respect in demonstrating added value. He offers a number of ways in which this can be done. By measuring the effectiveness of our PR activities we can then debate and discuss what is going right and what is going wrong and therefore decide what should be changed.

3   Thirdly, good business practice can be achieved by monitoring articles in the *People Management* journal and identifying good practice, and by noting and committing to memory some relevent studies.

4   Finally, and perhaps most powerful, is the learning that candidates can gain by sharing information. Working as a member of a team is better than the individual working alone. The People Resourcing examination is non-competitive, so groups who are following the programme of study can work effectively together and support each other's learning by sharing good practice.

One of the most effective ways in which the course leader/ learning facilitator can help is by structuring classes so that the learning process becomes a shared event.

The aim is to create an environment where students are able to access the curriculum (Performance Indicators, Knowledge Indicators and Indicative Content) by bringing to the class their own experiences through tutorials and effectively 'peer teaching'. In this way all can share in good, and sometimes reflect upon bad, practice.

There are of course practical, legal and ethical issues associated with this process. From a practical standpoint the course leader has to facilitate the process by setting the scene and making time for presentation and subsequent discussion.

Ethically some of the issues discussed may involve practices and perhaps outcomes relevant to individuals and individual firms, governmental organisations etc, so there has to be a shared understanding that discussion and debate is confidential within the confines of the classroom. Individual students have to be relied upon to sanitise presentations so as not to break confidences with clients and customer groups and also not contravene the Data Protection Act.

2   Evaluate existing PR processes, systems and procedures, and propose cost-effective improvements

This Performance Indicator is woven throughout all the major activities within the scope of PR. There is a need to manage an organisation, and the quality of the administration that supports the management activity can significantly affect the bottom line. Taylor (2002:7) quotes the following activities that can significantly affect the business if the supporting procedures are not cost-effective:

- human resource planning
- job analysis
- developing competency frameworks
- drawing up job descriptions, person specifications and accountability profiles.

Pragmatically the individual cannot do everything, so there must be processes and systems in place that generate challenge and perhaps cause a review of current practice. These could range from internal or external audits of sections of the business to including the responsibility for systems reviews in the individual's performance objective for the coming year.

In preparing for examinations, the student is advised to follow the practice described above for Performance Indicator 1. Which processes and systems have been introduced that deliver what the customer wants quicker and cheaper, or perhaps offers more choice and flexibility? Using the processes of sharing information, as mentioned above, students are encouraged to work together, to share good practice, to track events in *People Management* and to discuss and debate issues during class. Clearly, students need to be proactive in identifying and recording events that reflect this type of change. Quoting in part from Taylor (2002:xv) this entails:

- keeping in touch with the outside world, not just in the sector where you are working, in order to pick up ideas of performance improvement

- sustaining an open-minded attitude to innovation, so that ideas are not merely or automatically rejected . . . focusing on the constructive application of ideas

- understanding their organisation's strategic direction, goals and objectives, plus their role in contributing to the attainment of these purposes

- networking with customers, both internal and external, in order to keep in touch with the business, seeking out feedback and learning lessons from it

- proactively developing (or contributing to the development of) service innovations that yield customer advantage

- acknowledging that compliance is not a sufficient yardstick for measuring the effectiveness of the personnel/HR function and that corporate contribution is a more relevant indicator.

3   Optimise the available tools and techniques in the field of information technology (IT) (including the Internet) for all aspects of PR

Item 8 of the Indicative Content covers this Performance Indicator. Globalisation trends and advances in IT are driving today's business. Consider the following quotation by Göran Lindahl, the then chief executive officer of ABB, in 2000 (quoted in Joynt and Morton 2000:61):

> If talent is one side of the global competitive equation, information systems / technology (IS/IT) is the other. . . the two areas which will have the highest impact on our operations for the next five years are human resources (HR) and information technology (IT).

Knowledge indicator 8(1) covers the application of IT to the PR processes. Indicator 8(2) is about where to obtain information about IT systems, benchmarking etc.

Of interest in the context of this book is the application of IT (e-HR) to PR business processes. We can think of this in two ways:

1 the use of IT (e-HR) systems in support of internal HR processes

2 the introduction and impact of IT (e-HR) systems to replace, or to operate in parallel with, traditional PR processes that interface with the outside world (recruitment, selection, information sources etc).

Focusing on item 1, the implications for study are understanding how IT systems are employed and how they can replace traditional paper-based systems. The bigger question is what is, and possibly could be, the impact on PR practice and the way the HR professional goes about his or her work. This is not limited to how we can use IT (e-HR) and deciding what is best practice, but goes further, to consider the wider implications for the way HR supports the business now that knowledge and information can be distributed in such a readily accessible and interactive form, potentially 24 hours a day, 7 days a week. Already global business is applying this technology in PR activities and assessing further new ways how best to use this increasingly reliable and flexible technology (Taylor 2002:23–7).

In some ways, item 2 is more straightforward because it deals with the practice of using IT systems to replace traditional practices in recruitment and selection, etc. The innovative ideas that web-based technology offers in terms of, for example, selection testing cannot be ignored. The PR practitioner is expected to know where IT systems are used, and their advantages and disadvantages. This is a moving target, so relying upon textbook information to maintain a currency of practice and awareness alone is insufficient.

Embracing all practice that involves IT systems are the compliance requirements of the Data Protection Act (DPA). The HR professional is expected to know the fundamental requirements of the DPA and how to apply good practice, so ensuring regulatory compliance.

4 Assist with the design, development, implementation and review of PR methods to resolve specific corporate scenarios

Representative samples of this Performance Indicator are given as: geographical relocation, new business development, management of an acquisition, corporate restructuring, graduate/expatriate appointments, delayering, devolution, decentralisation, retrenchment and using an outsourcing partner such a recruitment agency.

This Performance Indicator is included because the HR professional is likely to face, at some time in his or her career, some big-picture activities and should therefore be prepared to tackle the fall-out from decisions to embark upon one or more of the above major scenarios, and be able to guide the management response to HR issues.

Clearly, the student cannot and will not be able to consider every possible contingency and successively reflect upon and research responses to each event. One can, however, consider some, if not all, of the scenarios, research good practice and transfer relevant practice and processes in response to the unknown. This is where the 'thinking performer' and all that this concept represents kicks in. It is about transferring knowledge and relevant practice and applying one's intelligence to solving related problems – 'Intelligence is what you do when you don't know what to do,' says Jean Piaget.

Candidates are expected to be able to apply themselves to the practical aspects of, for example, a downsizing exercise. What is good practice, what are the legal requirements in terms of consultation and preparation of redundancy terms, offers of alternative work, etc? Hand in glove with these process-driven activities there are the issues that arise when deciding upon identifying outplacement contractors. Candidates need to be aware of applicable and good practice in this type of field. However, having once worked through an example and read through and explored case studies in class, candidates should find that the concept is readily transferable to other unrelated but similar scenarios.

5   Undertake the full range of day-to-day functions for which the PR professional generally is accountable

Specifically, the range of functions alluded to above depends upon the industry sector in which the professional operates, but there are the core functions for which all PR professionals are accountable:

- recruitment
- performance
- reward
- retention
- release.

This is the 'knitting' of our business. These are the areas where there is a need to be aware of innovative practices that save time and effort and give service options but also to demonstrate competence in their selection and application.

Section 5 of Indicative Content details what this means in respect of the recruitment and selection activities; however, the analysis can be applied to each of the five core activities and so gives guidance on how we should approach preparing for the examination:

- *the background*: criteria for administration, considerations of alternative process options.
- *the processes*: principal methods, features, benefits and disadvantages
- *measurement of effectiveness*: techniques for monitoring outcomes, currency and relevance of processes, compliance and continuous improvement.

In essence this is the detail of how the PR professional goes about his or her business. Candidates will be expected to know the key processes, together with applicable theory and background, and should commit to memory examples of good or innovative practice and appreciate the relative advantages and disadvantages of the competing processes. For example, Torrington, Hall and Taylor (2002:174–87) offer an excellent window on recruitment issues, covering in a succinct manner the options and their relative merits. The increasing focus is on informed opinion, so candidates should be able to offer supporting theoretical evidence stating relevant reference sources.

6 Contribute to human resource plans that relate to and achieve business/corporate goals

Sections 1 and 4 of the Indicative Content detail, in the main, the coverage of this Performance Indicator. Traditionally HR planning has been associated with the large corporate enterprise or public-sector organisations, and the 'hard' statistical analysis of HR data, which essentially was demand forecasting – staff retiring, staff under development and training, numbers to be recruited. Typical examples of this are the macro-planning for teacher recruitment and training based upon demographic trends or the need to provide extra social facilities as urban populations change. There is still a need for this type of analysis, but the context of HR planning has changed.

Taylor (2002:70), quoting Mintzberg (1994), puts the case against HR planning, but candidates should be aware that there are equally powerful cases for HR planning (see Taylor (2002:73).

Planning in the context of PR covers a wide scope. There is a need for an outward focus to understand the external environment and the context in which business operates; this would include analysis of demographic trends, the political arena and social trends, eg the increasing demand for a recognition of the work–life balance and how this type of social change is (April 2003) reflected in legislation with the introduction of 'family-friendly legislation'.

There is also requirement for an inward focus to ascertain the current status of the business and trends of manpower utilisation over time. Collating this data is no good unless it is analysed and interpreted to assess what it means for the business in terms of PR, and then put it to some practical use, perhaps to inform managers that they have a problem in staff turnover. Having the capacity to identify the specific department where this is occurring is adding value by providing information, not speculation. Gone are the days when personnel crunched the weekly data taken from time cards. Using modern, and relatively inexpensive, management information systems, the tracking of key administrative information like staff turnover and absence is well within the scope of the smallest business. When considering the broader, longer-term perspective, data can be used to inform decisions on recruitment, training and development, staff-cost forecasting, redundancy, collective bargaining and accommodation (see Taylor 2002:76).

Considering the impact of different business scenarios on the requirement for staff, 'Contingency Planning' (see Taylor 2002:81–2) better informs all aspects of the PR process, from succession and skills planning through to the recruitment and release of staff.

Measuring today to plan for tomorrow

Candidates need to get to grips with the basics of the hard side of HR planning:

- indices and how they are used:
  - labour Turnover Index
  - stability Index
  - profitability or cost per employee.

(These indices can be applied to all or parts of the business.)

- methods of trend analysis:
    - cohort analysis
    - census method
    - cetention profiles.

With this type of information better decisions can be made in support of future business plans, and it can also be used to interpret, with some objectivity, what is happening, and has happened over time, with respect to employee stability/turnover.

In addition to the above factors, which, on a day-to-day level, can be used to inform the effectiveness of current activities, there is a need, at a higher level of practice, to analyse the alignment or 'fit' of HR strategies with the overarching business strategy and objectives. If a business's objectives seek to include the development of teamwork and knowledge management, then the reward strategy must reflect these requirements by rewarding effective teams and practices that encourage the dissemination of knowledge throughout the business. There is a need to analyse the 'fit' of HR policies, practices and strategies to ensure that they are holistic and make a coherent whole with overall business objectives and strategy.

Leading and supporting 'Change Management' requires a thorough understanding of how the business works. This means not only the interlinking structures and communication links but also how politics and power are used to bring about both desirable and undesirable outcomes. Although many think that political behaviour can be damaging to a business, Senior (2002:174) recognises it is a fact of life, a given, that 'power politics' will be a game played by some, if not all, of those involved. Planning is the first step to change, and the reality is that some form of political behaviour will manifest itself during the change process. The HR practitioner should be aware of how power and politics play their part in bringing about change.

Contribution to business planning

Once again the focus is on value-adding. Being prepared to contribute to business planning ensures HR and in particular the PR practitioner a place at the table where strategic decisions are made.

Above we saw how understanding what is happening in the business by measuring current activity – the *inward focus* – enables the practitioner to make informed decisions on the progress of activities, efficiency and effectiveness, and thus contribute to problem-solving and the development of business plans, and also the strategies to deliver the plans (see Figure 2 overleaf).

Figure 2: Contribution to business planning by outward focusing

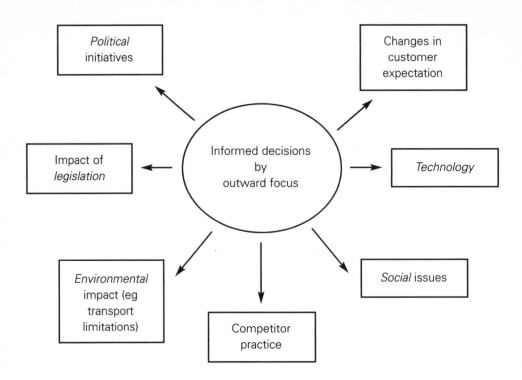

Figure 2 represents what would, in traditional change management, constitute a PESTL (Political, Economic, Social, Technological and Legal) analysis of the business environment – refer to Senior (2002:15–16) for a full discussion of the PESTL or PETS analysis. However, it is a 'PESTL analysis plus', because the outward reflection and analysis consider further influencing factors that impinge on business planning.

Softer planning issues

Performance Indicator 6 is a statement of the 'HR territory' or HRM business model, which was first presented by Beer and Spector in 1984 and became known as the 'Harvard Model' of HRM. Later modifications were made that reflect better the non-North American socio-political and business environment, eg David Guest's model of HRM, although arguably not ideal, embodies the fundamental concepts (see Beardwell, Holden 2001:19–21). Candidates should be aware of these models and their seminal influence on the development of HRM.

7 Critically evaluate PR systems and new approaches or methodologies

From a practitioner's viewpoint the annual budget exercise is enough to cause a flurry of activity and a proportional amount of navel-gazing about what PR activities the HR function will be involved with and in during the coming year. There is a requirement to answer three fundamental questions:

1   What PR activities will the (HR) function be involved with in the coming year?

2   What will they cost (as activities)?

3   What will be the implications for (HR) manpower?

Taylor (2002:ch15) deals with the costing of activities, calling this chapter 'Demonstrating Added Value'. It is a good place to start thinking about the costing processes if, for no other reason, because they form part of the annual planning cycle. Once it is known what activities will be entered into during the next planning period (all linked into the overall business plan and strategies), and what it costs to perform these activities (rituals?), we can then begin to understand where significant cost centres lie and so be in a position to decide to do something about it.

As an example, Taylor (2002:385) conducts a cost-benefit analysis in which he costs a series of work experience programmes for school leavers and then compares the outcome of this exercise, in terms of numbers recruited as a direct outcome of the experience, with the traditional cost of recruitment via newspaper advertising. This type of cost-benefit analysis, although simplistic in nature, is also a very powerful tool for the 'legitimisation' of decisions made or yet to be made.

The above analysis applies quantitative measures to the evaluation process, but candidates must also consider that decisions are not always so simple, and decisions based on a mix of quantitative and qualitative measures are generally the norm. Depending upon circumstance, issues such as reputation are as important as the saving of a few thousand pounds.

Candidates in the context of this Performance Indicator are expected to be able to break activities down into their cost elements, as described above, and to apply average rates for contractors, room rental etc. This in turn implies that candidates are aware of going rates for contractors, hourly or daily rates for administration work, etc. So often, when asked to cost an activity, candidates omit the administration costs and, when asked why, the response more often than not is along the lines, 'Well, the administrator is already in place, so there are no cost implications.' This implies that there is no 'on cost' to the business for this activity. This is a fallacious argument because, in reality, administration costs should be considered as 'opportunity costs'.

People Resourcing: the future

Previous examination questions have specifically tested candidates' awareness of the wider and longer-term picture, which may be coloured by social or legislative events. Indicative Content 10 gives some examples of issues of which candidates should be aware and above all have considered in terms of the impact they may have on their business, business sector and thus PR processes.

As a candidate and PR professional, how does one address this requirement? Is it asking too much? The simple answer to the second question is no, it isn't asking too much. One would be quite upset if, upon visiting a doctor or primary care practitioner, he or she was using practice and theory that was outdated and was not aware of current thinking and trends in medicine. By a similar token we cannot expect to maintain the respect of those who work for us, our peers and those who work for them if we (the PR professional) are not maintaining a currency of practice and awareness of the wider present and future issues that may have an impact on the way business functions.

The Indicative Content mentions:

1 debates over the future of work and employment, especially in view of continuing technological change, globalisation and the growth of e-commerce (and e-HR)

2 the dilemma of seeking to reconcile the interests and preferences of individual employees with the requirements and expectations of organisations

3 new thinking and research on topics relevant to PR such as:

 • matching personality types or learning styles with specific occupational roles

 • the effectiveness of psychometric tests

 • Emotional Intelligence

 • Knowledge Management.

4 actual and potential developments in employment legislation and other compliance arenas.

How does one prepare for this in the context of the PR examination? There is no 'cure all' response to this question, say by homing in on key topics. One can, though, consider the process offered and discussed in Performance Indicator 1 as not only good examination preparation but as a process that would inform continued professional development.

8 Co-operate positively with executive / managerial stakeholders – 'customers' – in the design and implementation of resourcing processes

This Performance Indicator reinforces two roles:

1 that the PR professional is responsible for a key function that demonstrably affects the bottom line. The role, by definition, carries managerial weight, and therefore it is incumbent upon PR managers/business partners to communicate effectively on issues, plans, strategies, processes and policies to relevant stakeholders.

2 that the PR professional is, at the same time, also performing as a service provider, and therefore there is a notion of accountability to those for whom that service is provided.

Item 2.2 of the Indicative Content identifies the stakeholders and the need to develop working relationships with those involved:

- managers with devolved accountabilities for people resourcing

- outsourced contractors

- recruitment agencies and executive search consultants, outplacement agencies, etc.

9 Advocate and ensure compliance with all appropriate ethical and legal obligations associated with PR

The detail of the requirements of this Performance Indicator are provided in section 9 of the Indicative Content.

Comments on legislation

Candidates are expected to know and understand key legislation and, above all, how it is applied to the PR process; this is the added value the PR professional brings to the table.

Legislation includes that generated both in the UK and from the European Union. Much legislation surrounds issues of discrimination, whether direct or indirect. Below is a list of fields of which the PR professional should have a working knowledge:

- Human Rights

- Disability Discrimination

- Equal Opportunities

- Race Relations

- Data Protection

- The employment relationship (recruitment, selection, contracts of employment, discipline, grievance, dismissal issues, etc)

- Health and Safety.

Ethical and professional considerations

Ethical considerations also play a significant part in today's business practice. Friedman (1963), quoted in Torrington *et al* (2002:25), posits that business should focus on 'doing business' within the 'rules of the game' and the law, and it is not the responsibility of the manager to engage in the promotion of social and therefore ethical issues.

This is not the stance of the CIPD – for two very good reasons.

The first is the recognition that business does not operate in a vacuum but in the world in which we live and 'do business'. Business ethics should, therefore, reflect the higher societal values and norms of this society. It is about being a good citizen. This is not to imply that the HR practitioner takes an evangelical stance and is a beacon of righteousness. Rather, the stance has to be pragmatic, honest and fair when choices have to be made.

The second reason that good, fair, ethical practice cannot be ignored is quite simply a hard-headed business reason: not to do so can negatively affect business effectiveness and profitability. Stakeholders in the business, external and internal, consciously or subconsciously reflect upon business practices and make their decisions about the company. A perception that employees are treated fairly reflects upon the ability to attract new employees; the perception that employees' contribution to debates and issues is considered and incorporated into corporate reflections, and so influences the higher-level decision-making, encourages employee commitment; recognising that diversity can positively lever business opportunities and that tribunal cases, for example those dealing with equal opportunity issues, are costly and, at the same time, damage business reputation, is a 'bottom line' issue that cannot be ignored. The notion of the 'critical *success* factor' is common in the language of today's business but there is also a need to be aware, as expressed in the Indicative Content, of those issues that would neatly go under the heading of 'critical *failure* factor'.

None of the above should imply that HR practices should reflect a 'softness' in business practice. The HR manager, or in our case the PR business partner, when dealing with his or her management colleagues, has to be respected and valued for the contribution made to the decision-making process. Candidates should be aware of examples of good practice, perhaps from *People Management* case studies, where business ethics has positively or negatively affected business outcomes.

10 Apply the principles and practice of Continuing Professional Development (CPD) for their own personal development

Because this Revision Guide specifically focuses on preparing candidates for the CIPD examination in *People Resourcing*, the topic of CPD is not addressed in this text.

• FURTHER GUIDANCE TO CANDIDATES FROM CIPD EXAMINERS

■ Demonstrating competence

To understand how to approach, to prepare for and to answer People Resourcing questions one needs to understand what the examiner is searching for in terms of the demonstration of skills, knowledge and application of intelligence (to apply the knowledge and skills).

To understand how CIPD examiners assess People Resourcing answer scripts one has to consider the objective of the process, which is to develop individuals to become PR professionals: that is, individuals who can operate in sometimes difficult and quickly changing business environments and who have shown themselves to be capable of meeting the exacting Performance Standards of the Institute. In essence, examiners, after marking each script, reflect upon whether the candidate has met, in an overall sense, the standards required by the CIPD.

Examiners use a three-part assessment framework:

1 Consideration of responses to questions in the context of the CIPD vision of the HR professional as a 'business partner' and 'thinking performer'

Consider, for example, the questions posed in Section B of the paper. Typically, the Chief Examiner puts questions from Section B of the People Resourcing paper in the form of a request to a PR business partner from a senior executive or line manager. The response is judged in two ways: in terms of the accuracy and relevance of the information provided and in terms of the quality, ie applicability, of the response. Candidates are expected to frame their responses in a manner that demonstrates their knowledge and understanding of the CIPD's core and what are termed BACKUP competencies (see below). These competencies are presented in the following bullet points:

2 The five 'BACKUP' competencies

- i Business orientation
- ii Application Capability
- iii Knowledge of the relevant field
- iv Understanding
- v Persuasion/Presentation skills.

3 The 10 core competencies

These can be found in Part 7 of the Introduction to the CIPD Professional Standards documentation (*The Vision for the new Professional Standards and for the Competencies*):

    i Personal drive and effectiveness

   ii People management and leadership

  iii Business understanding

  iv Professional and ethical behaviour

   v Added-value result achievement

  vi Continuing learning

 vii Analytical and intuitive/creative thinking

viii 'Customer' focus

  ix Strategic thinking

   x Communication, persuasion and interpersonal skills.

Convince the examiner

It is not good enough simply to regurgitate facts. Candidates:

- have to convince the examiner that they can add value by interpreting the information provided and even, when supported by relevant evidence or debate, show a willingness to challenge conventional wisdom or even research findings

- are encouraged to add to the debate (as raised by a question) by giving examples, making statements of 'fact'; wherever possible, statements should be reinforced by citations from appropriate third-party reference sources

- should be able to exhibit a well-informed understanding of the practice of HR outside their own immediate organisation and business sector, and should not be narrowly focused on ethical/legal compliance as the ultimate measure of HR performance. The PR professional should be seen as active and *not* passive in the role.

Some practical considerations – before and during the examination

Preparing to answer a case study

There is no definitive way to answer this type of question. The author can pass on to readers 'what works for him'. They can then make up their own minds what works for them! For 'something to work' implies that practice is essential. Individuals need to practise their skills at answering case studies within a specific time limit.

So, what works for the author? Consider the following process:

1 Scan-read the whole of the case study.

2 Carefully read the questions, highlighting or underlining the parts of each question that demand an answer.

3 Reread the case study, highlighting the parts which are pertinent to answering the question(s) posed.

4 Formulate a structured response in your mind.

5 Bullet-point the headings, in line with the structure you have thought about, on a 'scrap' part of the examination paper.

6 Commit to writing your response on paper. If the question asks for a report then you must write a report that includes title page, contents page, and section headings, perhaps with numbered paragraphs if this is applicable. From the examiner's viewpoint it is useful if you link the sections on the contents page with the questions posed.

7 As described previously – reread the question and then check back that the responses do in fact answer the questions.

Time management during the examination

The examination is of two hours' duration, with ten minutes given as reading time. Time is of the essence so candidates are advised to consider a 'game plan'/examination strategy.

The examination is in two parts, Section A, a case study, and Section B, which involves candidates answering seven from a possible ten questions. The suggestion is to give equal time to Section A and Section B. The implications are:

- Which section should be answered first? This is a difficult question and very subjective. Experience and discussion with colleagues who assist candidates to prepare for the People Resourcing examination tend to suggest that Section A should be tackled before Section B. The reasoning is not scientific but does have a certain logic. Time management is of the essence, so getting to grips with Section A, within the time allowed, forces the candidate, when moving on to Section B, to consider that there are seven tasks to be completed within a maximum time of 60 minutes. Leaving Section B until last emphasises the need to apply perhaps a more rigorous control over time allocation for each individual question.

It is very easy to 'go over the top' and spend more than the allocated 8 minutes when answering a Section B question. It is so tempting to be carried away and write an extended response to a Section B question because the subject matter is within the candidate's knowledge and / or experience comfort zone. When this happens valuable time is thus eaten away, which should have been productively used answering other questions.

- Having only 8 minutes to answer a section B question means that there is very little thinking time (a) to select which questions to answer and (b) to think about how to approach and answer the question. The suggestion is to scan-read the whole of Section B, ticking those questions that you believe you can readily answer; and mark those that you definitely consider to be at the bottom of your selection list, leaving those in the middle ranking. Proceed to answer the questions you have ticked within the 8 minutes allowed, in the order they appear in the paper. Once you have completed these questions go on to your middle-choice questions.

The implications of this strategy are to reinforce the message that time management is of the essence. Candidates need to practise and hone their skills, both at answering case studies and the smaller Section B-type questions.

Do not, when answering Section B questions, write greetings and introductions as though you were answering an e-mail (if the question was in the form of an e-mail) or end your response with some form of salutation. Simply answer the question, in a logical and factual manner, and move on to the next.

Time pressures, especially after two hours in an examination room, also affect the quality of handwriting. Examiners are not expecting candidates to produce copperplate text; they simply wish to be able to read what candidates have written, so help your examiner to help you by writing legibly.

Teachers and lecturers who assist/coach People Resourcing candidates are urged to spend tutorial time working through case studies and typical Section B-type questions. Mature candidates, especially, may not have sat a formal examination for some time (maybe years), so recommended practice is that one mock practice examination, under examination conditions, is conducted during the course of study.

General comments

Before attempting a question, read it thoroughly and identify the key areas that the examiner is asking you to address and thus to respond. Answer the question *asked*, not the question you think has been asked! Try to make life easier for the examiner and get him or her on your side. Consider simple matters such as the use of abbreviations: good practice for the first time you employ an abbreviation is to write the meaning in full, followed by the abbreviation.

• PRACTICE EXAMINATION QUESTIONS

This chapter presents examination questions from:

- May 2003 examination – complete paper, plus

- Further practice questions of equivalent standard.

■ Examination criteria

Time allowed: 2 hours, plus 10 minutes' reading time.

Candidates are required to answer Section A and seven of the ten questions in Section B.

Equal marks are allocated to each section of the paper. Within Section B, equal marks are allocated to each question.

Questions may be answered in any order.

If a question includes reference to 'your organisation', this may be interpreted as covering any organisation with which you are familiar.

The Case Study is not based on an actual organisation. Any similarities to a known organisation are accidental.

You are likely to fail the examination if:

- You fail to answer seven questions in Section B, and/or

- You achieve less than 40 per cent in each section.

■ PDS People Resourcing Examination – May 2003

Section A – Case Study

It is permissible to make assumptions by adding to the case study details given below provided the essence of the case study is neither changed nor undermined in any way by what is added.

Industrial Mecanica de Salvador S.A. (IMS) is a family company situated in Salvador, Brazil, manufacturing circular valves mainly for the country's oil industry. Some years ago the company's Chief Executive Officer (CEO) decided to make some changes in his company's traditional paternalistic, command-and-control structure in order to introduce a more participative management approach. A quarterly profit distribution plan was introduced, whereby 7.5 per cent of net profits would be paid to employees in proportion to their salary levels, and another 7.5 per cent distributed evenly to all employees. Thus even the lowest paid staff received a significant share of the company's profits.

The results were electrifying. Within weeks of the first profit distribution, a cost reduction programme and an in-house training scheme – aimed at improving the skill base of the employees and upgrading the quality of the firm's products – had been introduced by the workforce themselves. Antagonistic personnel attitudes and poor working conditions gave way to a climate of co-operation and improvements in the employees' cultural, emotional and spiritual lives.

At a recent quarterly meeting, two machinists complained that their supervisors took too long to respond to requests for help. A 30-minute debate ensued, after which the employees' assembly proposed to eliminate the role of supervisor, replacing it with the job of 'consultant'.

Although hesitant at first, the employees now feel free to call upon the best 'consultants' whenever they have a problem. The 'consultants', in turn, have an incentive to provide a quality service to their 'clients' because, if they don't, they have no right to be in the factory.

The general feeling at IMS is that quality of life, including life in the workplace, is reflected in the quality of the product. It is also accepted, moreover, that a right to a share is accompanied by a share in responsibility in the case of any losses. At IMS workers help absorb the company's losses, when they occur, by deferring overtime payments and occasionally accepting short-run wage/salary reductions. Clearly, however, none of this can happen without frank and open information sharing – transparency – which helps everyone's understanding of the company's performance, its activities, and its future strategies, costs, and profits.

You are the human resources (HR) manager in a similarly sized yet hierarchical, conventional, UK-based manufacturing company, which is currently in difficulties. Your CEO, Dr Tomkinson, has read about the experience of IMS and has even visited the company's plant in order to see for himself. Believing the IMS model to be your own firm's ultimate salvation, he is determined to introduce an IMS-type culture in his own company.

With this in mind, Dr Tomkinson has asked you to present proposals to address the people resourcing implications. At the same time, he recognises that it may not be entirely straightforward to transfer all aspects of the IMS experience into your own firm, and because of his own research background he needs to be reassured that there is convincing evidence to support any claims you make.

Produce a report for your CEO which addresses the following issues:

1   the lessons (from both research and organisational experience) about the problems associated with a shift of people resourcing philosophies, procedures and practices from those currently found in your own company to those which characterise IMS, plus some evidence-based proposals about how to make the changes easier to accomplish and assimilate

2   the methods of implementing the new philosophy with specific regard to replacing existing supervisors by 'consultants', namely:

   •   the proposed competency framework for the consultant role

   •   the selection methods to be used

   •   the actions to be taken in the case of existing supervisors who do not wish to become 'consultants' or who lack the necessary attributes.

In all cases, you should give reasons for your proposals, and your recommendations should be reinforced with references to relevant research material and benchmarking evidence from other organisations that may have undergone similar transitions.

[*Your report should give approximately equal attention to each of the above two issues.*]

Relates to Indicative Content as below:

Q1A

   1   People resourcing in context passim

   3   Approaches to people resourcing, especially (2) new paradigms

   7   Special-case scenarios

Q2A

   2   The strategic significance of people resourcing

   5   Recruitment and selection

Section B

Answer SEVEN of the ten questions in this section. To communicate your answers more clearly you may use whatever methods you wish, for example diagrams, flowcharts and bullet points, so long as you provide an explanation of each.

You should assume that having arrived at your place of work, you have just switched on your PC and the following ten e-mails appear on your screen. You are required to indicate the content of your proposed response; the method by which you transmit your response (e-mail, face-to-face discussion, etc) need not be specified.

1 **From a friend employed in the human resources (HR) function of another organisation:** We're thinking about the introduction of a performance review system with rating scales. I am uneasy, however. What does research say about the problems with rating scales and about how such problems can be overcome?

   Relates to Indicative Content 6: People management, Developing and improving performance.

2 **From your mentor:** I know that you're preparing for your CIPD exams, so here's a question for you. Anderson and Shackleton (1993) list many reasons why selection interviews have been attacked for their poor predictive validity. What do you think are the main ones? Explain why the selection interview continues to be so popular in your own organisation.

   Relates to Indicative Content 5: Recruitment and selection, especially (3) The selection process.

3 **From your HR Director:** Managers frequently tell me that someone working for them is 'good' at their job, and when I ask them what they mean they can't tell me. How do you define 'good' in this context?

   Relates to Indicative Content:

   1 People resourcing in context

   3 Approaches to people resourcing

   6 People management

4 **From the Sales & Service Director:** We're shortly going to search for people to work in our new call centre, and we think we should be looking for extroverts. However, I thought I should check with you before we start. Do you think we are on the right lines, or do you have any better advice – preferably delivered from authoritative research evidence?

   Relates to Indicative Content:

   1 People resourcing in context

   4 Human resource planning

   5 Recruitment and selection, especially (1) The background to recruitment and selection, and (2) The recruitment process

   6 People management

   7 Special-case scenarios

   10 People resourcing: the future, especially (2) The dilemma of seeking to reconcile the interests and preferences of individual employees with the requirements and expectations of organisations, and (c) New thinking and research on topics relevant to people resourcing.

5 **From the Finance Director:** Your function has already over-spent on its recruitment-advertising budget, so it's time to consider new approaches. I have a feeling that e-recruitment could be more cost-effective – what do you think?

Relates to Indicative Content:

> 5 *Recruitment and selection, especially (4) Measuring the effectiveness of recruitment and selection*

> 8 *Support tools for effective people resourcing, especially (1) The nature, scope, costs, benefits, and applications of information technology*

> 10 *People resourcing: the future*

6 **From a Business Unit Manager (Retail Outlet):** As you know, we don't have our own HR team, so I am dependent on you for keeping me up to date. I understand last month (April 2003) that some new employment rights came into effect. Can you summarise and explain the main ones for me, please?

Relates to Indicative Content:

> 9 *Compliance and ethicality obligations in people resourcing*

> 10 *People resourcing: the future, especially (4) Actual and potential developments in employment legislation and other compliance arenas*

7 **From a journalist working for *People Management*:** We're planning a feature about women in organisations, and our start point is the claim by Herminia Ibarra (*Financial Times*, 7 December 2001) that 'No world-class company has solved the problem of retaining and promoting women.' Even where women are hired at equal-entry levels in equal proportion to men, that 50 per cent dwindles to less than 10 per cent at senior levels. What practical steps could an organisation take to address this situation?

Relates to Indicative Content:

> 4 *Human resource planning*

> 10 *People resourcing: the future*

8 **From the IT Manager:** Something caught my eye the other day – I was reading an article about the learning organisation. The authors claim that the secret lies in the 'mix' between practices and people. What did they mean?

Relates to Indicative Content:

> 1 *People resourcing in context*

> 2 *The strategic significance of people resourcing*

> 6 *People management*

> 10 *People resourcing: the future, especially (3) New thinking and research on topics relevant to people resourcing, such as ... knowledge management.*

9 From the Chief Executive Officer: What's all this I keep hearing about a 'war for talent'? What's the evidence?

Relates to Indicative Content:

> *1 People resourcing in context*
>
> *3 Approaches to people resourcing*
>
> *4 Human resource planning*
>
> *7 Special-case scenarios*
>
> *10 People resourcing: the future*

10 From the HR Director: In October last year, the government launched a consultation paper on widening the scope of the Working Time Directive, and I read in *People Management* that some commentators are calling for a statutory 35-hour week. OK, this may not happen, but can you please outline the implications for people resourcing if it did?

Relates to Indicative Content:

> *4 Human resource planning*
>
> *9 Compliance and ethicality obligations in people resourcing*
>
> *10 People resourcing: the future, especially (4) Actual and potential developments in employment legislation and other compliance arenas.*

End of examination

■ PDS People Resourcing Practice Examination

The following Section A and Section B questions have been taken from previous examinations, some set under the PQS scheme and some in the June 2002 Specimen People Resourcing examination, or else they have been developed by the author. But all are representative in style, content and standard to the level required under the new PDS scheme.

Section A – Case Study (November 2002)

It is permissible to make assumptions by adding to the case study details given below provided the essence of the case study is neither changed nor undermined in any way by what is added.

Katherine and Peter Lim are two Singapore entrepreneurs who have successfully pioneered the Beautiful Living retail chain across the Asia Pacific region. Modelled originally on Anita Roddick's Body Shop, The Beautiful Living Empire nonetheless has a number of distinctive features that have given it a competitive advantage of its own. Firstly, the Lims both hold strong ethical views (they are practising Christians), and the openness of their business practices has often been contrasted favourably with the dubious claims made by the Body Shop about, for example, animal testing. Secondly, the Lims have not attempted to emulate the high personal profile pursued by Anita Roddick: instead, they have remained in the background, leaving their franchise holders to act as ambassadors for their values. Thirdly, the Beautiful Living group has diversified its products and services so that it now offers health and fitness programmes, health foods/drinks, stress management therapies, work–life balance counselling and a general framework of lifestyle enhancement activities.

Now it is time for Beautiful Living to enter the European market place, initially by opening 50 retail units in the UK. The company's worldwide Internet sales have already convinced Katherine and Peter Lim that there is a potential in the UK, and they in turn have persuaded a group of Malaysian investors to provide the investment to enable the project to get off the ground.

Because the success of Beautiful Living so far has been largely attributed to the firm yet unobtrusive leadership offered by the Lims, they intend to play a major part in ensuring that things go right from the start. Each of the 50 retail outlets will be operated by a franchisee, carefully chosen to ensure an appropriate mix of ethicality and business acumen. Each franchisee will be required to supply a personal investment of £100,000 but will be guaranteed a generous share of profits.

Management of the franchise process will be meticulously detailed to ensure total conformity with the Beautiful Living brand image. Staffing is considered to be a key ingredient for the maintenance and projection of this image, but as the vast majority of the franchisees will have no direct experience of recruitment, selection or staff management, and will not have access to professional help (especially in the early stages), it is essential that they are given clear guidance on how to proceed.

Katherine and Peter Lim have commissioned you to produce the 'People Resourcing Guidelines', which will become part of the instructions issued to all Beautiful Living franchisees. Present your draft proposals for these guidelines, under each of the following three chapter titles:

1   how to select the right people for Beautiful Living

2   how to avoid the legal pitfalls associated with recruitment and selection

3   how to get the most out of the people you employ.

[You should devote approximately equal amounts of time and space to each of the above requirements.]

Section B

Answer SEVEN of the ten questions in this section. To communicate your answers more clearly you may use whatever methods you wish, for example diagrams, flowcharts and bullet points, so long as you provide an explanation of each.

You should assume that having arrived at your place of work, you have just switched on your PC and the following ten e-mails appear on your screen. You are required to indicate the content of your proposed response; the method by which you transmit your response (e-mail, face-to-face discussion, etc) need not be specified.

(AQ) Author Question
(SP) CIPD Specimen Paper, June 2002

An e-mail from a business collegue arrives reminding you:

1 As a senior HR business partner of a consulting firm you were asked for your understanding of the term 'Knowledge Management'. Briefly indicate your response and indicate five ways in which the HR department could support knowledge management within your business.   (AQ)

From the Personnel Director of your Trust hospital:

2 National Health Service Trust Hospitals have experienced and still experience difficulties retaining and recruiting sufficient midwives. There has been a steady loss, from the service, of competent staff who have found it more 'accommodating' to work as agency staff rather than as direct employees of the NHS. Current estimates indicate that there is a shortfall of in excess of 5.7 per cent of midwives across the UK and of 6.3 per cent in England (The Royal College of Midwives: Evidence from the Review Body, 2002).

What would you consider are the options for improving the position in our hospital?

• in the short to medium term?   (AQ)

3 Working in central London as an HR business partner to a company employing some 500 workers, many of whom are employed in virtual customer relations departments, responding to e-mail, telephone and fax communications, you are constantly beset by recruitment and retention problems.

You have been asked by one of your line managers to review the 'informed' options:

• to reduce staff turnover

What would your response be to this request?   *Similar* to May 2002
                                    Employee Resourcing PQS Examination (AQ)

From your HR Director

4 Some research suggests that good-looking people and those with optimistic and enthusiastic attitudes and a sense of humour are more likely (a) to get jobs and (b) to gain career advancement. What are the psychological principles involved in this phenomenon? What are the dangers for our management?

From the Operations Manage:r

5 New legislation affecting the Data Protection Act (DPA) comes into force this year, 2003.

Prior to our forthcoming recruitment exercise can you, as our HR adviser, conduct a short awareness seminar on the key relative aspects of the DPA for line managers who will be involved in the process.

Please detail the key advice you would give our managers about the activity to ensure that the process is orchestrated in a fair and transparent manner. (AQ)

A reminder from your HR Director on the progress of work you have agreed to do:

6 As HR manager of an operating company of a large multinational organisation you are requested to assist the CIPD in some work they are preparing on the 'Management of Expatriate Staff'. They are interested in your 'informed' views as to what factors you would identify as the **'six key ingredients'** for effective resourcing policies and practices related to the assignment overseas for employees. (SP)

From your CEO:

7 I'm speaking next week at a CIPD seminar on "The Future of Work". Brief me on four major trends that will affect working patterns in the UK over the next five years. (SP)

From your CEO:

8 Appraisals are about continuous performance improvement. If your appraisal system doesn't achieve this, chuck it out,' robustly claims Mary Budd (quoted in *Management Today*, December 2001). Your comments, please, so far as the system used in your own organisation is concerned (May 2002)

Prior to going to make a presentation at a local CIPD branch, your Personnel Director asks for some advice:

9 According to the available research evidence, what are the best ways of predicting whether a candidate will perform successfully in the job or not? Give reasons for your views. (May 2002)

From a fellow CIPD student working for a local authority:

10 Have you read about the government's campaign to improve public services? My council wants to be proactive about this, so how can we ensure that our resourcing practices reflect what the government wants us to do? (SP)

End of examination

• FEEDBACK ON EXAMINATION QUESTIONS

■ PDS People Resourcing Examination – May 2003

Section A

Strictly Confidential – draft proposal

Tomkinson Quality Machine Components

A Vision for the Future – a turnaround strategy

A report compiled by A G Candidate

Section A

Section			Page
	Contents page		2
A	**Background summary**		3
B	**Vision for the future**		4
C	**Implications for the future**	**1** Communication and Change Plan	5
		1.1 Draft process for change	5
		2 Roles & Responsibilities	5
		3 New Competencies	6
		4 Recruitment & Selection	6
		5 Practical & Legal Considerations	7

Examiners, please note:

QA part 1 is answered primarily in Section A + Section B, B1 of the report

QA part 2 is answered primarily in Section B2 through to B5 of the report

P2

Report Section A – Background summary

Changing the culture of a company is probably one of the most difficult tasks to achieve. There are a number of models that can be called upon to help bring about the desired change. Barbara Senior, in her book *Organisational Change,* and Charles Handy, who has written a series of texts about organisational change, have greatly added to the general understanding of the change process.

Classically, we have to understand where we are in terms of our people resourcing (PR) environment and consider where we would like to be. We can then understand the differences between the future (desired state) and the present, and so better bring about the change.

Our company can be characterised as hierarchical, with differentials between management technical and manual labouring staff. The company is unionised and with a generally good employee relationship. The unions mainly become involved during the annual pay negotiations or whenever, for example, there is a grievance or disciplinary action.

We have operated in the same location for the past 30 years and are generally perceived locally as a 'good' employer. Recruitment tends to be from the local labour market, traditionally the sons and daughters of our existing employees. We are known as a family business. This has its advantages and disadvantages. To improve our competitive position, you have indicated that we need to introduce new technology; concomitant with the technological change we perhaps also need to attract some better-qualified talent, especially technicians and engineers, so our recruitment net needs to be expanded. As you know, we have seen new competition come into the market from overseas and slowly chip away at our customer base.

There is a need to do things differently, but whatever we do has to 'fit' into the organisational paradigm on which we would like to build.

Report Section B – Vision for the future

What type of organisation would we like to build that will take us forward for the next 10 to 15 years? Consider the accompanying table, which has been quickly put together. The management team can add further meat on the bone but the drift is clear.

P3

Table 1: Today & Tomorrow

Current situation	Future vision
Management processes closed and secretive	These processes will truly have to be open and managers will have to 'walk the talk'
Direction from supervisor (management-led)	Overall direction from management but intermediate goals by self-motivated teams
Supervisors decide when/how work is accomplished, task-specific	Teams and individuals become empowered to make these decisions
Promotion to supervisory/management initially through technical competence	Supervisors become facilitators/consultants
We are very hierarchical	We will probably have to restructure with a flatter organisation – so that organisation reflects the way we wish to communicate
Recruitment focused on technical competence	Technical competence is a starting point for recruitment, basis to be considered by us – key recruitment decisions need to be based on fit, largely associated with interpersonal skills
Training and development – largely management-directed	Individuals and teams need significantly greater say in their development
Performance management – annual appraisal, largely management-led, focus on delivery of hard targets	More involvement of staff in the process (design also?). Need to recognise and to focus on softer issues of people leadership, good teamworking, and of course rewarding teams rather than individuals

The table is incomplete: for example, nothing has been said about remuneration practices that could/should be adopted.

There has been a recent article in *People Management* (Vol.4 No.1 8 January 1998), entitled 'Profitable Personnel', by Michael West, of Sheffield Hallam University. It details what happened when a UK company embarked upon a programme of improved employee involvement in the workplace and the resulting positive outcomes. This would be a good starting point to consider the practices we could usefully employ to bring about the change we desire.

P4

Report Section C – Implications for the future

1 Communication and change plan

To make the changes possible we will have to communicate effectively, at all levels, and to involve all our staff in the process. Consider the following draft communication plan (after Kurt Lewin): management and supervisory staff will have to be 'brought on board' at an early stage, once the management team have agreed the direction that we need to take. All management and supervisors will have to be trained in how we wish them to communicate with their people and so start to live the message. Once we have the management on board we would then need to bring in the unions and explain to them the situation we face, our plans and our strategy.

1.1   Draft process for change:

1   Explain the current situation and engender an understanding of why we cannot continue in the way we do business.

2   Deliver our vision for the future and elicit feedback. We need to take notice of this feedback by using the feedback suggestions from staff, so perhaps put together a change team from different parts of the business (start as we mean to go on) facilitated by a quality consultant (from outside).

3   Take note of the feedback and develop a plan of action with various groups in the organisation.

4   Start to bring about that change by restructuring/delayering – whatever we decide.

5   Start to train staff how to work in teams, to help them understand what is expected of them and at the same time move to finalising the design of the business.

6   By this time, it will be necessary to roll out some of the interim outputs of the change and elicit more feedback – communication needs to be regular and informative (pragmatic).

7   Complete the change process and start to work on any of the issues that have arisen.

8   Finally – test the 'temperature' to see how (if) things are beginning to embed.

2 Roles and responsibilities (QA part 2)

Above all, you, as CEO, will have to champion the change. Total commitment from your management and supervisory team are vital for this major change event to stand any chance of working. A culture change is very difficult, but not impossible, to bring about.

In some respects our supervisory, especially first-line, management staff are going to be the most affected by these stages. They will probably feel that they are losing status and self-respect, as well as perhaps a myriad other feelings. Some, of course, will be aware that other firms in this sector have been successful in going part-way in the

P5

direction that we intend to go and have embraced the changes. Others will not be so keen and will feel threatened. We must make time to explain these changes to all our people. Not all, however, will be able to make the transition from supervisor to internal consultant.

The move to becoming an *internal consultant* does not mean that the individual is a 'yes' man or woman; rather, he or she is someone whom I would expect to be able to make value judgements based on informed opinion and make recommendations based on logic, not on what people want to hear. This has implications for our management staff. Some of our senior managers are also going to have to address their interpersonal skills and, for example, not take personal issue with a challenge to a decision or proposal they may have made. People will have to think differently and work more co-operatively as part of a team.

3 New competencies

Can I suggest the following list of knowledge, skills and attributes (KSAs) that we would expect our consultants to exhibit? Technical competence – in whatever area they working in – opens the door to becoming an internal consultant but does not guarantee entry. However, they will all be required to have or to eventually develop mastery of the following competencies:

- good interpersonal skills, empathy, understanding
- personal confidence/strength of character
- resilience in fighting one's corner
- good negotiation skills.

The above is an incomplete draft. We should involve our staff in helping to decide what sort of framework would best suit our desired culture.

Too few of our people really understand our business or the environment within which it operates. So, added to the above we could seek to develop a broader understanding of the business in all our managers and consultants (by increasing learning, job rotation . . .).

4 Recruitment and selection in Tomkinson Quality Machine Components

This could be better achieved by using assessment centres with some situational exercises etc as the selection vehicle. We already have *some* people who probably fit into the type of consultant role that we envisage, and, together with our change consultant, we could put some meat on the assessment programme.

For new staff we would have to consider seriously how to recruit and select, but again use the assessment centre approach. The consultant role will be instrumental in the facilitation of teams. We could manage a blend of internal development of our existing staff who meet the profile, plus graduate/professional recruitment.

Note: Assessment centres (Smith, quoted in Taylor (2002) are one of the better predictors, but expensive. However, for this type of role it is so critical it will be worth the expense.

5 Practical and legal considerations

This is a 'nutty one' to answer, but our circumstances are such that we cannot shrink away from our responsibilities. The options are:

- limited opportunities for redeployment – with retraining in other roles
- some of our staff could be offered early retirement
- redundancy with outplacement support.

From a legal standpoint, we should consider that there could be some redundancies from this change 'exercise'. We would have to declare an at-risk situation in accordance with current employment law. The unions by this time will have been brought on board so the process will be a formal recognition of the facts, but we would have to work with all involved parties.

I consider that staff would have to apply for their jobs under the new organisation. We could ring-fence certain areas, so focusing on those staff at risk, should they have appropriate knowledge, skills and attributes or be trainable. Each individual who applies will be treated on their own merits.

P7

Section B

Q1

In essence, many, but not all, of the problems are associated with the person performing the appraisal. Appraisers tend to focus their ratings around the mid-point of the scale (*skewed central tendency*) and not use either the 'excellents' or the 'poor/weak' indicators, those points at the ends of the scale. Scales are too woolly, with terms like 'good', 'average' etc, there being insufficient definition around the scale points. Some appraisers also consider how (they thought) they did the job and mark current incumbents down.

How can it be improved? By training and by holding workshops to achieve a mutual understanding of the issues and measurements involved, so bringing about a more unified standard. Some companies, especially large mature operations, bring in a forcing function which restricts the grading, so that, for example, 10 per cent of staff are rated as excellent, 30 per cent are very good and the remainder are satisfactory, with some poor performers. The rankings, before being finalised, are reviewed by a peer management group where at least two managers/supervisors must know the person being assessed.

> Comments: In this question candidates were expected to answer both parts of the question; what are the issues and how can they be solved (or at least ameliorated)?

Q2

Stephen Taylor (2002) lists the major reasons that interviews have been attacked for their poor predictive validity. In his work, he quotes Smith *et al*. The major reasons have been listed below:

- the similar-to-me effect – looking for someone in one's own image

- the self-fulfilling prophecy effect – where the interviewer has asked questions that will naturally lead to a desired conclusion

- the prototyping effect – the interviewer has gone into the interview with a pre-programmed expectation of the type of person he or she would like to see in the job

- the halo-or-horns effect – the interview is affected by personal appearance

- the expectancy effect – where the CV has unduly influenced the interviewer's perception of the candidate

- the personal liking effect – no comment.

Interviews remain popular despite their poor validity (below 0.3) because, for those conducting them, there is a high degree of face validity: managers like to be involved with the recruitment of staff who will work in their department. Moreover, many interviewers fallaciously consider that they are excellent interviewers.

Comment: Candidates are not asked how they can improve the interview process, but one can imagine that this could form the basis of a similar question in future papers. Stick to what has been asked, because time is of the essence. Some, not all, of the bullet-pointed responses, have attracted comment to explain their meaning. Those that are sufficiently self-explanatory have been left with no comment. This is an individual's 'call' when answering the question.

The author has not systematically answered with all the possible options as described in the core text (Taylor, 2002:173–4) because the answers provided here are an attempt to reflect what is expected in an examination, given the restrictions of time.

Q3

What does 'good' mean in the context of work? Does it mean 'competent' or perhaps 'effective in terms of delivering goals and objectives' (CIPD studies by Guest and Purcell)? This can be related back to the CIPD's concept of a 'thinking performer'. Explicit in this is having an understanding of the essential knowledge for the role, the skills to be able to deliver and the ability to reflect upon the options and decide upon a course of action, and so apply the knowledge and bring about a desired outcome.

Added to the above is the notion of going beyond contractual terms or the constraints of the job description – what has elsewhere been termed OCB (Organisational Citizenship Behaviour), to deliver and to meet customer requirements and to accept personal responsibility for outcomes.

Perhaps we should be thinking of process definitions rather than a definition that focuses simply on results, because the route to achieving an end is often as important as the result.

Comment: Of course, some may define 'good' in other ways, eg purely in terms of the individual's compatibility with his or her peers and group/team members. In general, however, a definition of the adjective 'good' in this context is likely to provoke some discussion of the 'thinking performer' concept as above.

Q4

The evidence suggests that extroverts are *not* appropriate for call-centre work: they talk too much, they are poor listeners, they become bored quickly, and then they either leave or start behaving mischievously.

So what type of person is best suited to this role? It would be preferable to seek mild introverts with a low superego in a work situation (so that they can put up with constant rebuffs, if that happens to be the nature of the call-centre activity), a high level of interpersonal skills and certainly a measure of what Britannic Assurance calls 'altruism', ie the willingness to think of situations from the perspective of the other person. Do not let age be a factor here, because more mature people are likely to be more settled and not have unrealistic expectations of the role/interaction with the public.

Comment: This is one of those questions where you either know the required response or you do not know it – there is no half way. This type of question makes the choice easy – to include or exclude from your list of questions to answer during your initial assessment of Section B.

Q5

Initial investigations suggest that e-recruitment might *not* be the panacea for which we are all looking. There are a number of relevant factors to be taken into account: e-recruitment only works efficiently when the organisation has a significant number of posts to fill across a large geographical area, eg graduate trainees, sales representatives, the military and so forth. Because e-recruitment encourages applications from manifestly unsuitable candidates, some form of electronic screening must be deployed.

For e-recruitment to work, moreover, potential applicants need (a) Internet access and (b) awareness of our e-recruitment initiative. Neither of these can be taken for granted, unless the company is an employer 'brand', eg Cadbury Schweppes, Asda and the like. We are not in that league, so we would probably need to source any Internet recruitment to a specialist agency, which again militates against sole use of this type of vehicle for recruitment. Presently we advertise in specialist journals for our professional staff. These organisations tend to have their own electronic jobs board, as do the newspapers in which we advertise.

So, to sum up, I don't think that we can go it alone with simply having our own Internet site – we wouldn't be able to attract the people we need. But we do need to invest in our own system, because this is the way business is moving. We will still have to rely upon agencies, and press advertising, for the foreseeable future.

Comment: Candidates should be aware of the advantages and disadvantages of all forms of recruitment and selection processes.

Q6

Many of these new rights are concerned with the employee's ability to seek the opportunity to work flexibly, especially for working parents with children under the age of 6 and those who have children with disability under the age of 18.

If a request is made, the organisation must respond within 14 days, and there is only a limited number of grounds on which a request for flexible working may be refused.

It is associated with the government's response to encourage firms to develop family-friendly policies. We are reasonably ahead of the game, so to speak, in this respect because of our *Work–Life Balance* initiative, which is in line with current government thinking – the DTI (Department of Trade & Industry) website gives more details.

Comment: Again this is one of those questions where you either know the required response or you don't, so it could be easy to include or exclude from your list of questions to answer during your initial assessment of which Section B questions to tackle.

Q7

The 1998 WERS survey (Cully *et al* (2002) confirms that women are still under-represented in senior managerial positions. The fact that they constitute circa 50 per cent of all employment positions is due in the main to their significant representation in part-time employment and clerical, service-type work. This issue is part of the management of the larger issue of the management of diversity.

Research shows that more women voluntarily leave employment earlier than their male counterparts owing to concerns about balancing work and family life. Couple this with the social 'work issue' that women have still to break through the glass ceiling – one needs only to read the recent high-profile tribunal cases involving discriminatory practices against women – and there is no wonder that female representation diminishes by the time women are ready to move into senior management positions.

A number of options are open, specifically:

- Improve family-friendly policies, flexible working and home working for periods of time, career breaks and job share. Government legislation goes some way to force employers in this direction.

- Change cultures, which positively encourage diversity (Shell intends to have 20 per cent of its senior executive positions filled by female staff by the end of 2008 – *People Management*). Many large businesses have appointed 'Diversity Directors' to raise the level of this issue and at the same time give a clear, positive message (Ford Motors, for example).

This, in reality, is not just a moral issue but also an economic necessity. One could argue perhaps too little too late!

> Comment: This type of issue will not go away, and candidates are advised to track the People Management journal for related articles on diversity, labour market trends (and the reasons – demographics etc) and the options open to business, together with examples of initiatives taken. Candidates should also be aware of the WERS survey (see References, page 89), which is conducted every four years, the last published version being the 1998 census of UK industry.

Q8

The issue raised (re the learning organisation) relates to what is currently understood to be Knowledge Management and Intellectual and Social Capital theory (John Storey has written at length about this topic).

In essence, this theory states that it is simply not good enough to employ intelligent and individually motivated people (Intellectual Capital): we must also bring about a sharing of knowledge by processes that encourage this activity.

We can recruit people in the type of image (knowledge, skills and attributes), that we as a company value; we must then put the processes in place (Knowledge Management) that further encourage a sharing of knowledge and thus corporate learning. Even our performance management systems must reflect what we are trying to achieve. It is about the 'fit' of processes, so that when 'bundled' or aligned together they all form part of a coherent HR package. Generating piecemeal initiatives will usually cause confusion and produce no meaningful benefits.

> Comment: Understanding the key issues of what is meant by Intellectual Capital, Social Capital, Knowledge Management and Emotional Intelligence is key for today's PR professional.

Q9

The evidence for a 'war for talent' is highly ambiguous. It is real in the case of organisations that operate in a highly competitive, highly innovative, knowledge-based environment, where the concept of 'human capital' does make sense and where competitive advantage is largely attributable to a very small number of 'core competents' (often only 1 per cent of the total workforce) whose expertise is very rare and who, therefore, could not be easily replaced.

The idea of a 'war for talent' is less relevant for organisations functioning in a relatively stable and even non-competitive environment, since the need for innovation in such enterprises is far less self-evident.

The above description focuses on the types of individual, but the issue cannot be divorced from the 'tightness' of the labour market.

The implications for us are that we should be identifying those who have the skills and knowledge and be considering the options (for development, retention, etc) in terms of HR planning. There was a short article in *The Times*, 30 March 2003 about Capital One Bank's approach to people development and selection for senior posts. They positively identify their talent and have a long-term plan in place to develop them.

Comment: In essence, the second, third and fourth paragraphs in the above response answer this question. Given a little time it is always useful to say what the implications are for the business; I decided that I had time, so I made some suggestions, since I had the boss's ear!

Q10

We, in the UK, have some exemptions from the Working Time Directive; junior doctors are one such group. Staff can also opt out of some of the restrictions at present, but this might change (Taylor, 2002).

If nobody were allowed to work more than a 48-hour week or, even more stringently, a 35-hour week, there would of course be some consequences, because we would have less time to get the job done, given that the business would probably not wish to increase staff numbers. (France has introduced this legislation – to reduce unemployment.)

In essence, business would:

- probably start taking more interest in people productivity, multiskilling and so forth

- probably show greater reluctance to employ full-time or even part-time people

- instead engage fixed-term contract workers (at a higher level, organisations would be likely to use consultants rather more).

The consequence is that people in the labour market with no identifiable skills would find it much harder to gain employment, and to that extent it is likely that differential rewards within organisations may become more pronounced.

Comment: There are clearly a number of options open to management should legislation be changed. This type of question offers candidates an opportunity to demonstrate their ability to think around the subject and give considered views about likely outcomes based upon informed opinion. One needs only to go back to David Guest's model of the HRM environment and Atkinson's model of the flexible firm to obtain a 'directional steer'.

End of examination

■ PDS People Resourcing 'Practice' Examination

Section A

Recruitment and Selection for Beautiful Living –

A draft proposal

<u>A report compiled by A G Candidate</u>

Report Contents

Section			Page
	Contents page		2
A	**Management summary**		3
B	**The recruitment and selection process**		4
		1 Managerial Positions	4
		2 Assistant Positions	5
		3 General Comments	5
C	**Training of the selection team**		6
D	**Legal considerations when recruiting and selecting staff**		6
E	**How to get the most out of people**		6

Examiners, please note:

QA1 is answered in Sections A, B & C of the report

QA2 is answered in Section D

QA3 is answered in Section E

P2

Section A – Management summary

For each shop or group of shops, there are two distinct roles that have to be resourced:

- Shop Manager
- Sales Assistant

After discussion with the franchiser and franchisees, agreement has been reached on the selection criteria. These will be based on a number of key competencies, both skill and behavioural (essentially select for attitude and train for skill) coupled with previous relevant experience. Having the relevant experience (for either role) will be the first hurdle that candidates will need to overcome.

All candidates, whether considered for the shop manager or sales assistant role, will be expected to have a similar ethical outlook in terms of respect for others (cultural considerations) and to be open and frank yet sensitive. The objective is to develop teams that are self-starters, so it is important to identify candidates for the management position who would be comfortable *working towards* a facilitator or coach role.

To assist in the process of recruitment and selection and future HR support, an outsourced HR function (eg Accenture Services) will be contracted to assist with the initial interview process and, under my direction, coach all involved staff. The HR contract agency will then provide HR support for all shops for a period of two years. A member of the HR team will be present at each location to assist and be present at all interviews.

Because the franchisees may have little experience in this sector of the retail business, the strategy will be to recruit staff with previous experience for all roles, until such time when sufficient competence has been built within the organisation before taking on inexperienced people.

P3

Section B – The recruitment and selection process

The recruitment and selection process will be carried out by the following means:

- Advertising in the local and regional press. Candidates will be sent a standard application form focused on the needs of the role, an accountability profile and a person specification based upon the competency profile developed with the Lims and the franchisers.

- Depending on the numbers applying for the roles, first-cut candidates will be telephone-interviewed, and those successful will be invited to attend face-to-face interviews.

- Selection will be by structured interview – note that because of the diverse location of the shops and the low numbers involved in each location, assessment centres are deemed too expensive. A franchisee trained in interview skills (they want to see whom they are recruiting), with myself or someone from the HR support contractors, will, as previously stated, be present at each interview.

1 Managerial positions

Part of the recruitment process was to ask candidates who were applying for the management position to indicate, in no more than a half to one page of A4 of typewritten script, how they would describe their management style and why they think it works. Candidates who have not managed people before but who have relevant experience will be asked how they would manage people and what type of problems they might envisage. For both roles candidates are requested to give an example of where their tact and diplomatic skills have been tested to their limits.

Behavioural traits

- Good communication and interpersonal skills, sense of humour
- Self-starter
- Sense of customer awareness and service
- Previous managerial experience in similar relevant environment or potential
- Tactful, diplomatic and pragmatic (good customer-facing skills).

Knowledge and experience (skills)

- Previous knowledge and experience of retail work
- Business-focused – understands the balance sheet and the need to deliver on targets
- Numerate and literate (written and IT)
- Has potential for development.

2 Assistant's position

Candidates will be asked to write, in no more than a half to one page of A4 of typewritten script, how they approach work – what motivates them in their work and what interest they get out of it, what they can bring to the role and why they are applying to Beautiful Living for a job. Candidates will be requested to give an example of where their tact and diplomacy have been tested to their limits.

Behavioural

- Good communication and interpersonal skills, sense of humour
- Self-starter
- Sense of customer awareness and service
- Ready to learn and try new things
- Tactful, diplomatic and pragmatic (good customer-facing skills)
- Has potential for development.

Knowledge and experience (skills)

- Previous knowledge and experience of retail work
- Business-focused – understands the balance sheet and the need to deliver on targets
- Numerate and literate (written and IT).

The skills required of the assistant are not unlike those required of the manager but clearly they are focused primarily on the customer.

3 Selection – general comments

The selection will be planned as follows:

- Psychometric testing – personality profiling; numerical aptitude; reasoning ability.
- Semi-structured interview (review application form and structured questions about hypothetical scenarios and personal experiences – the candidate's written A4 profile will be used as a starting point (did they write it?) for discussion).

Note: the profiling etc will have to be conducted by competent staff – it is expected that the HR agency will provide this facility. Feedback of the results will be provided to candidates.

P5

Section C – Training of selection team

Franchisees will be involved in the selection process, and therefore they will have to be trained in appropriate techniques. This will be done in a number of one- or two-day events around the UK and will address:

- interview techniques, need for good preparation, pitfalls of interviewing (biasing, halo effect, recruiting in my own image, temporal effects, etc), open/closed questioning techniques, role play etc

- legal requirements of recruitment and selection, pitfalls.

Section D – Legal considerations when recruiting and selecting

Prior to the awareness training day all staff involved in the recruitment and selection process will be given copies of the *People Management* 'How to . . .' guides and ACAS guides on recruitment and selection. Training will be given on issues relating to:

- questions associated with sexist and racist views

- disability Discrimination – access to interview facilities

- implications of the Data Protection Act – availability of interview notes, should candidates request to see them.

An HR specialist will be present at each interview to:

- provide a check and balance during the interview and sounding board after the event

- ensure legal compliance during the conduct of the interview.

Section E – How to get the most out of our people

This is about motivation and how, therefore, people are managed and treated. It is about:

- involvement techniques

  - communication – the Lims are very open, and so developing a communication system that is two-way and therefore involves staff in the business will be in line with the company mould

  - creating a culture that values people and their views

- performance management

  - which recognises the worth and 'developability' of individuals to contribute

  - which monitors and rewards progress in delivering objectives

  - which encourages staff to assimilate the behavioural characteristics of the firm

- encouraging teamwork and managers to become facilitators
- having a reward system that is part of the overall strategy of managing people and reflects the company's objectives of developing teamwork and sharing knowledge.

> *Comment: Clearly, more could be said on all of the above, but this must be balanced against the time constraints placed upon the candidate.*

Section B

Q1

My understanding of how we consider the issue of knowledge management is briefly laid out below. There was an article in *People Management* entitled 'Human Capital: a thorough evaluation' (April 2002) that is worthy of a read.

Definition: Concerned with people and the *interchange* of knowledge.

Five ways of supporting knowledge management:

1 Help to develop an open culture.

2 Promote a climate of commitment and trust.

3 Advise on the design of organisations that support the above.

4 Advise on resourcing policies that attract the people with appropriate skills and attributes.

5 Advise on methods of motivating people to share the knowledge – reward people within the appraisal/reward framework for sharing knowledge.

> *Comment: In addition to the above five elements, candidates could choose from those below:*
>
> - *Develop the performance management process, which supports the sharing of knowledge.*
> - *Develop processes for staff development that encourage knowledge transfer.*
> - *With IT (information technology), develop systems for capturing and codifying knowledge.*

Q2

How can we improve the position in the NHS with respect to midwives' retention and recruitment in the short-term?

- The short-term problems can be addressed by considering what pool of qualified staff are 'potentially available' to the Trust and how it can attract them back to work and hold on to them.

It has been suggested that there has been a significant turnover of midwives in recent years. If turnover has been high, then why have people left? Could it be the unsocial hours, or non-family-friendly policies and practices? There is a requirement to have a system that also finds out why staff are leaving. In this case the introduction of flexible working practices, coupled with the new salary package and the offer of pensionable employment, may encourage staff back into the profession from both agency work and from among those who have left to bring up children. As a stopgap, recruitment from overseas for such positions is also an option.

Critical to the improvement of morale is a concerted effort to bring the staff shortage under control.

The strategy to improve staff morale should focus on involvement techniques. Techniques that would strengthen the psychological contract between the employer and employee include: the management style – a move away from the autocratic style of management; considering new styles of working and perhaps moving to more involved ways of working; taking opportunities to consider methods of working – job enrichment, eg flexible teamworking, perhaps self-managed teams. The implication here would be a move from telling, shouldering the burden to facilitating, co-ordinating, sharing responsibility. Clearly, there will be a training and development requirement.

- For staff there will be a need to learn to work in teams and all that this implies. Consideration will have to be given to leadership techniques, budgeting and managing processes of work. Clearly, there will be a training and development requirement.

Also worth considering are: flexible times of working; developing a new appraisal system focusing on realistic objective-setting; personal development; improving communication – consultative committee (legal requirement), team briefings, etc.

Comment: This is a question where it is possible to 'over- egg' the response. It is important to remember that for each Section B question there is only approximately 8 minutes in which to formulate and make a response.

Q3

Measuring and attacking turnover

Activities associated with the above are a cost in themselves. However, knowing how your business 'works' is important when it comes to adding value. Standard ways of indicating turnover are given by Stephen Taylor (2002), where he talks about:

- **Wastage Index**
- **Stability Index**

Each is a way at looking at the problem from a slightly different angle.

The **Wastage Index** is the cruder:

= (Leavers over 12-month period/Total staff) x 100%.

The **Stability Index** is a little subtler, seeking to consider only those staff who have remained in post for (usually) 12 months – this acknowledges the fact that the highest turnover occurs within the 12-month period:

= (Number of staff employed for >12 months)/Original number of staff) x 100%.

As Taylor points out, 'a company can have high wastage & low stability', or as he says, 'worryingly, low wastage & low stability'.

It is important to understand what statistics mean; there are lies, damned lies and statistics.

Determining the reasons for leaving

- Exit interviews:

Consideration – Not having the interview conducted by line management, eg 'impartially' by personnel. For a number of reasons exit interviews are not the most reliable tool unless, of course, you are dealing with a very, very honest person. Timing is important – they should be done as soon as the person hands in his or her notice to leave. You may try using 'Separation Questionnaires' – these are anonymous and may be done by an impartial contract organisation.

It is useful, in all of the above, is to ask the individual directly how improvements can be made.

- Attitude surveys:

Rather than closing the door after the horse has bolted it is perhaps a better idea to survey staff before they take any drastic action – ie test the health of the organisation. *With attitude surveys it is useful to give staff feedback from the results – and perhaps what the business is going to do about any areas of concern.*

- Quantitative methods:

Useful for trend analysis, isolating rogue departments, sections, factories. Internal benchmarking. (External benchmarking can be quite difficult.) It is important to think through the type of statistics, choosing those that have relevance.

- **Surveys of ex-employees:**

Currently some large organisations are experimenting with requesting employees who have left the organisation to complete questionnaires within a period of months – probably done anonymously and by a contract agency.

Reducing staff turnover

The feedback (above) will give clues to a longer-term response to high turnover. The short-term reduction of staff turnover can be achieved in three ways:

- by recruiting people who best fit the company mould and can work alone, and those who are comfortable in their own company and confident about their own abilities

- by offering greater flexibility of working to existing staff.

Q4

Treating or perceiving the overall character of an individual in a positive or negative way results in a characteristic specified as positive Halo, negative Horns effect. We are also subject to 'stereotyping' individuals – eg 'All asylum seekers are terrorists.'

Managers should be aware of these 'traps' in the path of logical decision-making. The HR professional should properly brief those involved in the interview of the pitfalls of one's perceptions as described above. The interviewer should seek out facts.

The dangers for management are twofold. Firstly, the wrong people may be recruited or promoted because decisions were not made objectively, perhaps because there was no challenge process in place. The results of this type of error may not be instantaneous, but the outcome of such a poor decision-making process is reduced efficiency and possibly low staff morale. Secondly, there is the issue of discrimination/non-compliance with the relative sex, race or disability legislation, should there be a clear biasing in the selection process, whether intentional or unintentional. Non-compliance opens the door to costly litigation and a blemished reputation.

Q5

The Data Protection Act has been extended to cover all types of information, whether electronic or hard-copy data.

With respect to recruitment and selection:

- Take care with the application form – a one-size-fits-all approach may not be acceptable; the form may have to be designed to fit the recruitment activity. If age is immaterial, then why include this as a request for information?

- Feedback from third parties (references) should only be requested with the full knowledge of the candidate – to ask the general question 'Can we approach your previous employer?' may not be good enough.

- References – the DPA covers information sent and received. It is therefore a contravention of the Act to disclose the contents of a reference (usually given in confidence) to a third party. It would also be the breaking of a psychological contract of trust.

- It is good practice to nominate someone 'responsible' for compliance with the Act and associated company policies.

Q6

In respect of good practice when managing our international staff the key considerations should be:

- the reasons the expatriation is necessary – is the posting simply because of a technical requirement or is it a development posting (etc)? Candidates should be clear why they are being asked to go overseas

- cultural acclimatisation – before and on arrival at the overseas location

- the compatibility of the expatriate's partner to cope with an international assignment. The majority of failures of expatriations are associated with some form of discontent on the part of an accompanying partner. (Refer to the studies conducted by Sparrow *et al* of Sheffield University for the CIPD (*Globalisation and HR*) and also Black *et al* (1999)

- limited-term assignments

- financial rewards/compensation

- re-assignment on the expatriate's return to the UK

- availability of support from home country while on assignment – mentor, administrative link, etc.

Expatriate compensation should be well thought through and be considered part of a holistic expatriation package.

> *Comment: Candidates can write much on this subject. The task is to say just sufficient. There are a number of core texts on expatriation issues that reflect good practice. A good place to start is the CIPD's own study on expatriation practices.*

Q7

The following will be significant shaping factors over the next five to ten years. Refer to Barbara Senior (2002).

Probably there will be a continued impact from globalisation, a general decline in the work ethic and an increased interest from employees and other stakeholders (government, especially a Labour government) in the work–life balance. This is already apparent in recent (April 2003) legislation about family-friendly policies. The demographic trends will put pressures on recruitment, causing businesses to look more closely at hitherto overlooked pools of talent (ex-offenders, the unemployed, overseas). Further pressure will be caused by the general decline in population growth (zero), which will cause business to consider the options in engaging further an ageing population. Innovative practices must be employed – extending the retirement age, reducing restrictions on pension law etc. Having and encouraging diversity in the workplace will be key to success – ie further ethnic, sex or age integration, all coupled with greater flexibility.

Q8

Appraisals are about:

- assessing past performance against previously set targets (linked to the business plan)

- appraising performance, which can then be turned into reward measures

- setting future targets, hard and soft (linked to the balanced score card)

- associating some hard targets with output appraisal. More difficult to assess are targets associated with the softer, behavioural skills. These may be assessed through critical incident, customer feedback and peer feedback (360-degree feedback in essence).

- determining learning and development needs: refer to Beardwell and Holden 2001.

Criticisms about my own (imaginary scenario, in this case) organisation:

My biggest concern is that our management does not see/appreciate the importance of the appraisal. Typically, appraisal is conducted in a ritualistic manner: another box to tick, against which I, as a manager, am being assessed. There is a lack of ownership by management: the whole process is seen to be owned by HR and driven by HR. I would be happier to see this turned on its head and the process clearly owned by management, but perhaps administered and facilitated by HR. The current process is not adding to the business performance; rather, in its present form, it is adding to the administrative burden and so costing the business.

Q9

No selection method is entirely accurate, but some are better than others. The following is a rough guide to the accuracy of prediction.

- Assessment centre (promotion)

- Assessment centre performance coupled with personality tests.

The assessment centre is costly and time-consuming, and so is not broadly used. However, the skilled practitioner can embed in the programme psychometric exercises for a number of attributes ranging from personality traits and numerical aptitude to ability testing. Key, though, is linking the assessment centre to the company's core behavioural skills

- Work sample tests – in terms of the validity, these sit between the two types of assessment centre.

Work sample tests, in a similar way, show a candidate how to get an understanding of the work process and also how to make a judgement as to whether the work is appealing. Selection is a two-way process.

- Biodata

- Structured interview

Biodata is reliant upon large blocks of data about individuals who have made successes in particular jobs and careers. (It was first used by the US Navy for determining the most suitable persons to become deep-sea divers.)

Interviews and application forms are still significantly used by business, although research shows that their reliability is questionable. Taylor argues that although the classic trio of application form plus interview and references is questionably accurate, too radical a change may cause problems for candidates.

Because jobs change as time goes by, Taylor argues that it is better to screen people out who are lazy, lacklustre and dishonest and to recruit instead for attitude (difficult to work with – don't fit the culture) and ability (one may say potential).

Q10

The government's concern is about the need for local authorities to consider a broader church of attributes when considering people for jobs, including:

- behavioural questions in the selection process in order to test customer focus and orientation

- induction, training and development that concentrate on customer-facing behaviours

- reward and recognition systems that reflect achievement and the departmental goals, objectives and strategies

- role modelling and leadership from management

- involvement techniques to improve employee commitment.

A number of organisations consider the philosophy of 'select for attitude and train for skills'.

End of examination

• PERFORMANCE STANDARDS

■ Purpose

The pace of change affecting organisations shows no sign of slowing down, and has a strong impact on managerial expectations about:

- employee behaviour and attitudes
- corporate pressures on managerial performance
- the employability potential and aspirations of labour market entrants
- the criteria for success applied to those engaged in employee resourcing activities.

Therefore, this module is designed to recognise the following key points:

- For any organisation to achieve its people resourcing (PR) outcomes the PR professional must be aware of the organisation's strategic direction and be able to demonstrate that the resourcing policies, systems and procedures contribute to achieving the corporate strategic goals.

- There is no guarantee that today's organisations will exist in the indefinite future, either at all or in their present form. So this module seeks to address the competencies resourcing professionals are likely to need 'everywhere and tomorrow', rather than just 'here and now'.

- Administering employment systems in line with the law and recognised standards of fairness and good practice is important, but it doesn't make the difference between success and failure in the market place. PR professionals add real value through their contribution to the recruitment, selection, deployment, development and retention of people who themselves add value to the organisation, individually and collectively.

- Many employers still use recruitment and selection processes for which there is little or no supporting evidence. The talents and potential of people are often dissipated or neglected, poor performers are still ignored, sidelined, promoted or dismissed without any serious attempt to resolve the problem, and performance review systems generate passionate debate because they appear unable to generate significant benefits for the organisation or the employee. Many of those engaged in employee resourcing concentrate on minor incremental efficiency or system changes and on the legalistic, ethical and procedural dimensions of resourcing – instead of on the added-value dimension, where there is considerable scope for further improvement.

- The competent practitioner has to be familiar with the major tools and techniques related to PR, and also be able to assess the potential for using them, determine their suitability for specific organisational scenarios, implement them with and through the co-operation of other stakeholders, evaluate their effectiveness and carry out any necessary modifications.

This module crucially sets out to develop, demonstrate and assess these capabilities.

Performance Indicators

Operational Indicators   Practitioners must be able to:

1 Make constructive contributions to the development or enhancement of people resourcing (PR) policies.

2 Evaluate existing PR processes, systems and procedures, and propose cost-effective improvements.

3 Optimise the use of available tools and techniques in the field of IT (including the Internet) for all aspects of PR.

4 Assist with the design, development, implementation and review of PR methods to resolve specific corporate scenarios (representative examples are: geographical relocation, new business development, management of an acquisition, corporate restructuring, graduate expatriate appointments, delayering, devolution, decentralisation, retrenchment, using an outsourcing partner such as a recruitment agency).

5 Undertake the full range of day-to-day functions for which a PR professional generally is accountable (eg recruitment, performance, reward, retention, release).

6 Contribute to the development of human resource plans that relate to and help achieve business/corporate goals.

7 Critically evaluate existing PR systems and new approaches or methodologies.

8 Co-operate positively with executive managerial stakeholders – 'customers' – in the design and implementation of resourcing processes.

9 Advocate and secure compliance with all appropriate ethical and legal obligations associated with PR.

10 Apply the principles and practice of Continuing Professional Development for their own personal development.

Knowledge Indicators

Practitioners must understand and be able to explain:

1 The underpinning rationale for People Resourcing as a means for accomplishing corporate purposes, strategies and goals through people.

2 The environmental context in which PR is designed, operated, reviewed and improved.

3 The benefits, limitations and potential of existing and emerging methodologies in the generic field of PR.

4 The legal obligations governing the creation and use of all PR strategies, policies, procedures and systems.

5 Ethicality criteria for all key aspects of PR, including the benefits of compliance and the risks associated with its neglect.

6 The systematic approach to PR, from the creation of a cost effective human resource plan, through recruitment, selection, socialisation, training/ development, performance management, retention and review, to eventual employee release.

7 The nature, purposes, features, applications, benefits and disadvantages of the principal techniques for human resource planning, recruitment, selection, corporate socialisation and people performance.

8 The operational need for pragmatic PR programmes, in circumstances of organisational turbulence, crisis, closure or apocalyptic change.

9 New developments in PR and their application potential.

10 Contingency factors that influence the principles and practice of PR across and within various employment sectors.

■ Indicative Content

PR in context

The changing world of work and organisations:

1 The big picture: contextual themes relevant to PR (such as globalisation, privatisation, ecological/environmental concerns, technological innovation, accelerating 'customer' expectations, competitive intensity and demographic change).

2 The corporate picture: evolving employer expectations about employee behaviour and attitudes, with special reference to 'adding value' obligations; new forms of work contract; the PR significance of organisational transience.

3 The people picture: the future for the work ethic; processes of vocational choice; the job/career dichotomy; the concept of 'employability' and its implications.

2 The strategic significance of PR

1 The PR function: the key role of people as contributors to the realisation of corporate purposes, strategies and goals.

2 The 'customers' for PR: establishing priorities between various stakeholders and 'customers'; creating, sustaining and developing partnerships with internal and external stakeholders such as:

- managers with devolved accountabilities for PR

- outsourced contractors

- recruitment agencies and executive search consultants.

3 Managing their possibly conflicting and competing concerns, values and expectations.

3 Approaches to PR

1 The traditional paradigm: a coherent corporate strategy leading to effective human resource planning, recruitment and selection, induction, training and development, performance review management, employee retention, recognition and reward and release (voluntary or not).

2 New paradigms: the development of aspirational visions for people performance, contribution and commitment; systems that convert these visions into reality; PR practices in the organic enterprise.

3 Contingency-based PR: the specific features of PR processes that typically exist in each principal occupational sector (private/public/not-for-profit); variations from the traditional paradigm (eg for deliberately transient structures, in environments of extreme turbulence, or circumstances of organisational crisis).

4 Human resource planning

1 The rationale for human resource planning: its potential benefits, disadvantages and dangers.

2 Designing, implementing and reviewing the effectiveness of a human resource plan: the use of appropriate measures, eg employee retention, turnover, productivity, and profitability-per-employee.

3 Internal and external factors affecting human resource planning and implementation including:

- trends in the labour market (both supply and demand)

- competitor practices

- technological change

- political initiatives

- the social background

- enhanced customer expectations

- strategic clarity and consistency within the organisation

- corporate politics and the distribution of power.

5 Recruitment and selection

1 The background to recruitment and selection: criteria for administering the process efficiently and effectively; alternative approaches to managing vacancies; job analysis; job descriptions versus accountability profiles; person specifications versus competency frameworks.

2 The recruitment process: the principal methods available – their features, benefits and disadvantages (eg media advertising, the Internet, employment agencies, executive search consultancies).

3 The selection process: the principal techniques available – their features, benefits and disadvantages (eg interviewing, individual group simulation exercises, and psychometrics).

4 Measuring the effectiveness of recruitment and selection: techniques for monitoring outcomes to ensure continued business relevance, validity, reliability, and compliance: continuous improvement processes in recruitment and selection.

6 People management

Optimising commitment and performance:

1 Assimilating people into the organisation: the socialisation/induction process, transmitting corporate values and behavioural parameters.

2 Developing and improving performance: the benefits and limitations of appraisal; criteria for effective performance feedback; coaching, mentoring and other systems for achieving a productive balance between the employee's needs and the employer's requirements.

3 Dealing with performance issues: assessing the nature and causes of performance problems (eg absence, attitude, capability or output); the range of remedies/solutions available; techniques for implementing action and monitoring consequences.

4 Motivating people: the elements of job design; the principles underpinning cost-effective reward and recognition strategies.

5 Keeping people: practical policies for employee retention and commitment, especially where long-term employment is not guaranteed.

6 Releasing people: the effective management of strategies, policies, systems and processes for retirement, redundancy, dismissal, and voluntary turnover; mechanisms for preventing or alleviating problems where appropriate.

7 Special-case scenarios

1 PR policies, plans, processes and systems for particular (possibly short-term) corporate exigencies. Representative examples are:

- recruiting expatriates (temporary or permanent) or graduates
- choosing outsourcing agencies or recruitment consultants
- creating (new) shift work teams and patterns
- resolving resource problems in times of acute labour scarcity
- establishing new corporate entities arising from mergers or acquisitions.

8 Support tools for effective PR

1 The nature, scope, costs, benefits and applications of information technology (including the Internet) for recruitment, selection and the retention/retrieval of employee data.

2 External sources of information, advice and assistance, including the CIPD, published research and benchmarking indices.

9 Compliance and ethicality obligations in PR

1 The place of legal, ethical and professional compliance as a 'Critical Failure Factor' for PR practitioners and their employers.

2 The legal constraints and frameworks relevant to PR.

3 The influence of legal and quasi-legal directives originating through the European Union and elsewhere.

4 Ethicality expectations within each major dimension of PR, including diversity management, equal opportunities and discrimination.

5 Professionalism criteria: CIPD Codes of Conduct and publications from other sources.

10 PR: the future

Note: Practitioners – like practitioners in any discipline who are actively engaged in Continuing Professional Development – are expected to be up-to-date with emerging PR issues. The four here are representative examples only.

1 Debates over the future of work and employment, especially in view of continuing technological change, globalisation and the growth of e-commerce.

2 The dilemma of seeking to reconcile the interests and preferences of individual employees with the requirements and expectations of organisations.

3 New thinking and research on topics relevant to PR, such as:

- matching personality types or learning styles with specific occupational roles

- the effectiveness of psychometric tests

- emotional intelligence

- knowledge management.

4 Actual and potential developments in employment legislation and other compliance arenas.

• REFERENCES, BIBLIOGRAPHY AND WEBSITES

■ References

BEARDWELL, I. and Holden, L. (2001) *Human Resource Management: A contemporary approach.* London, FT Prentice Hall.

CULLY et al., (2002) *Britain at Work, as Depicted by the 1998 Workplace and Employment Relations Survey.* London, Routledge.

FRIEDMAN, M. (1963) *Capitalism and Freedom.* Chicago, University of Chicago Press.

HUCZYNSKI, A. and BUCHANAN, D. (2001) *Organizational Behaviour: An introductory text.* London, FT Prentice Hall.

JOYNT, P. and MORTON, B. (2000) *The Global HR Manager.* London, CIPD.

MAYO, A. Human Capital: A thorough evaluation. *People Management.* Vol 8, No 7 4 April 2002. pp36–39

MINTZBERG, H. (1994) *The Rise and fall of Strategic Planning.* New York, Prentice Hall.

SENIOR, B. (2002) *Organisational Change.* London, FT Prentice Hall.

STOREY, J. (2001) *Human Resource Management: A critical text.* USA, Thompson Learning.

TAYLOR, S. (2002) *People Resourcing.* London, CIPD.

TORRINGTON, D., HALL, L. and TAYLOR, S. (2002) *Human Resource Management.* London, FT Prentice Hall.

■ Bibliography

ARMSTRONG, M. (2002) *A Handbook of Human Resources Management Practice*. London, Kogan Page.

BACH, S. and SISSONS, K. (2002) *Personnel Management: A comprehensive guide to theory and practice*. Oxford, Blackwell.

BLACK et al. (1999) *Globalising People through International Assignments*. USA, Addison Wesley Longman.

BRATTON, J. and GOLD, J. (2003) *Human Resources Management Theory and Practice*. 3rd edn. Basingstoke, Palgrave.

GRANT, B. (2002) *Employment Law*. USA, Thomson Learning.

PILBEAM, S. and CORBRIDGE, M. (2002) *People Resourcing: HRM in practice*. London, Financial Times, Prentice Hall.

STOREY, J. (2001) *Human Resources Management: A critical text*. USA, Thomson Learning.

WALTON, J. (1999) *Strategic Human Resources Development*. London, Financial Times, Prentice Hall.

■ Useful websites

Acts of Parliament, UK general   www.hmso.gov.uk/acts.htm

Data protection

UK Data Protection Act   www.dataprotection.gov.uk.htm

Employment law

UK employment law   www.emplaw.co.uk/

Employee relations

Institute of Employment Studies   www.employment-studies.co.uk

Equal opportunities

Equal Opportunities Commission   www.eoc.org.uk/

European

European Union   www.europa.eu.int/

Statistics, trends

UK Government Statistics   www.statistics.gov.uk/

International Labour Statistics,
International Labour Office   http://laborsta.ilo.org

Trade unions

Trades Union Congress   www.tuc.org.uk

Other useful HR-related sites

ACAS	www.acas.org.uk/
Association of Online Recruiters	www.aolr.org/
CIPD	www.cipd.co.uk/
Learning and Skills Council	www.lsc.gov.uk/
Investors in People	www.iipuk.co.uk/
People Management	www.peoplemanagement.co.uk/
International Labour Organisation (useful website from drugs to statistics)	www.ilo.org/

INDEX

NOTES